Canyon Country Camping

Notice Regarding High-Use Areas

The Bureau of Land Management is considering management changes to reduce health hazards and environmental damage at high-use primitive camping sites near Moab. Proposed changes include constructing "minimum development" campsites with toilets and fire rings at popular primitive camping sites and providing dumpsters to serve high-use areas. Also camping at specific sites may be limited where necessary to avoid conflicts with day use or to allow vegetation to recover.

Cooperation with these management changes will help preserve the beauty of canyon country.

Cataloging Data:

Barnes, F. A.
Canyon Country Camping,
Revised Edition
1. Camp sites, facilities—Utah—Guidebooks
2. Utah—Description and Travel—Guidebooks
I. Barnes, F.A. Canyon Country Camping.
II. Title
GV198.L3
ISBN O-915272-34-2

Canyon Country Camping

A complete guide
to all kinds of camping
within the canyon country
of southeastern Utah

By

F.A. Barnes

Wasatch Publishers
1991

This book is number TEN in a series of practical guides to travel and recreation in the scenic Colorado Plateau region of the Four Corners states

All written material, maps and photographs in this book are by F.A. Barnes unless otherwise credited.

Sketches by Kathy Nunley

Wasatch Publishers
4460 Ashford Drive
Salt Lake City, Utah 84124

ISBN 0-915272-34-2
L.C. No.: 77-95041

Front Cover: Joint Trail, Canyonlands National Park.
Back Cover: Primitive camping near Hovenweep National Monument.

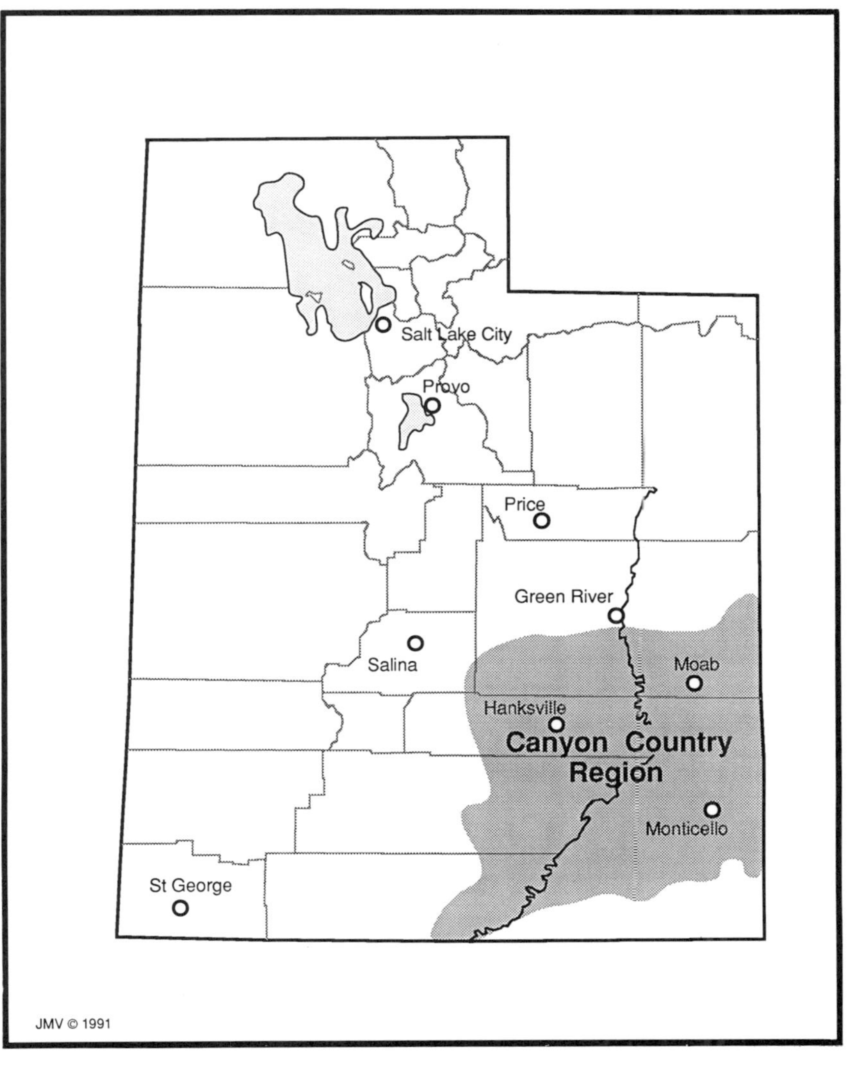

The Canyon Country Region

Contents

Reprinted By Permission of Bureau of Land Management and of Canyonlands Natural History Association

USING UNDEVELOPED CAMPSITES
ON THE PUBLIC LANDS

Published by:

Canyonlands Natural History Association

125 West 2nd South • Moab, UT 84532 • 801-259-6003

In cooperation with:

The Bureau of Land Management, Moab District Office

AN OPPORTUNITY FOR OUTDOOR RECREATION

Undeveloped campsites are found throughout Canyon Country on Public Lands administered by the Bureau of Land Management. Such campsites are located along rivers and streams, at roadside turnouts, under shady cottonwood trees, and at other desirable locations. Dispersed, undeveloped campsites are normally recognized by the presence of a fire ring. Such informal sites are popular with vehicle campers, jeepers, and hikers.

When asked why they prefer dispersed campsites, visitors cite the freedom to set up camp as they please, to camp with a large number of friends, to camp in an area where pets are allowed, or to camp without having to pay for the facilities found at developed sites.

DISPERSED SITES ARE OPEN TO THE PUBLIC

It is the general policy of the Bureau of Land Management that undeveloped Federal lands under its administration are available to the public for camping and general recreation with the following provisions:

1. that camping at any one site is limited to 14 days per visit.
2. that users pack out their trash.
3. that users avoid camping within 100 feet of springs so that water is accessible to wildlife.
4. that campfires not be left unattended.

GUIDELINES FOR USE

Canyon Country is being "discovered" by an increasing number of visitors. As a consequence, many campsites are showing signs of deterioration.

You can increase the ability of dispersed sites to accommodate successive groups of campers by adopting a minimum-impact style of camping. The following procedures have proven effective.

Camp at a previously used site if possible.

Research studies have shown that the most rapid negative changes to soil and vegetation occur during the first few times a campsite is used. If it is necessary to camp at a previously unused location, minimum impact camping techniques can reduce such impacts.

Maintain the beauty of campsites by staying on existing travel routes.

Avoid driving, riding, or walking over areas where the vegetation is intact. Many of the most desirable undeveloped campsites are surrounded by networks of tracks. Over the years, the vegetation around these sites has been greatly reduced, and in some cases, soil erosion is very noticeable.

Do not put cans, bottles, or aluminum foil into a fire ring.

These items do not burn, and their presence will lead subsequent users of the site to build a new fire ring.

Avoid building new fire rings.

Redundant fire rings scar the natural beauty of sites and reduce the amount of space available for sleeping and cooking areas. If the site you select already has trash in the fire ring, please clean it out and place the trash in a bag for proper disposal.

Use only dead and down wood for campfires.

Both dead and live trees add to the scenic qualities of campsites. Leave them for the next visitors to enjoy.

Burn campfire logs to ashes, then douse with water.

Do not smother a campfire with soil, as this will make it difficult for the next visitor to use the same fire ring. If you must leave a campsite before the fire burns all of the wood, douse the fire with water before you are ready to leave camp, then stir it with a stick to make sure it is completely out.

Garbage can lid used as a fire pan

Consider using a fire pan.

A fire pan is a metal tray or garbage can lid used to contain a campfire and prevent the fire from blackening the soil. Before breaking camp, it is a simple matter to transfer cold ashes into a plastic bag or other container for disposal at home. If you use a fire pan carefully, it is possible to leave a campsite with no scars or evidence of your use.

Dispose of human waste properly.

Solid body waste and urine should be buried in a hole six to twelve inches deep. The disposal site should be located well away from streams, campsites, and other use areas. Toilet paper should be placed in a small plastic bag and put into your camp trash bag.

Pack out your trash (and a little extra).

For years, public land managers have promoted the "pack-it-out" concept in an effort to foster a self-cleanup ethic among public land users. This program has generally been successful. Most people no longer leave or bury trash at campsites.

While the pack-it-out program has reduced the amount of trash left by campers and day users on the public lands, it has not entirely eliminated unsightly trash. You can take an additional step by picking up trash left by less thoughtful people. This act helps maintain the scenic beauty of your public lands and frees land managers for other work. Think of that extra bag of trash you collect as your contribution to maintaining something you enjoy: undeveloped recreation sites on the public lands.

YOUR PUBLIC LANDS — U.S.A.

USE - SHARE - APPRECIATE

5M-10/88

Camping opportunities are unlimited in canyon country. Colorado River with Behind The Rocks area and La Sal Mountains in the background.

Introduction

General Terrain

For the purposes of this book, "canyon country" is defined as the region of southeastern Utah bounded by Interstate 70 and U.S. 50 on the north, the western boundaries of Capitol Reef National Park and Glen Canyon National Recreation Area on the west, the northern Navajo Indian Reservation boundary on the south, and the Utah/Colorado border on the east, plus the eastern slopes of the La Sal Mountains that lie within Colorado. The map on page 5 shows this region and its approach routes.

Within canyon country, the terrain is quite diverse. The term "high desert" applies to much of it, but can only be used in a general sense because there are so many exceptions. In elevation the region varies between 3700 feet, the approximate elevation of the surface of Lake Powell, to 12,721 feet, the elevation of the highest peak in the La Sal Mountains. Between these extremes, there are vast areas of open desert broken only by occasional rock outcroppings, verdant valleys, elevated plateaus and three distinct and separate mountain ranges.

The more open country is walled and divided by thousands of miles of picturesque, winding bluffs and escarpments, and slashed deeply in many places by immense, complex and deep canyon systems, all of which ultimately drain into the Colorado River gorge that bisects the region diagonally. In addition to the mountains and canyons, the region is still further distorted and broken by many great uplifts and ridges, such as the San Rafael Swell and Comb Ridge, and ancient contortions in the earth's crust have left other surface irregularities such as grabens, salt valleys, anticlines, synclines, monoclines and folds.

Even though, climatically, the region is classified as high desert, the mountains and high plateaus are far from arid, and even the lower elevations contain several major and minor rivers, and countless perennial and intermittent streams and springs. The major rivers, the Colorado, Green, San Juan and Dolores, all originate in higher mountainous country outside of the canyon country region. The minor rivers, the Fremont, Muddy, Dirty Devil, Escalante and San Rafael, all originate within or very near the region.

In addition to rivers and streams, canyon country also has lakes. There are several small lakes in the Abajo and La Sal Mountains, and immense Lake Powell fills 180 miles of the Colorado River gorge and its tributaries above Glen Canyon Dam.

Human settlements and developments are few and far between in canyon country, and its total population is quite small. Relatively few highways and roads penetrate the vast region, and well over ninety per cent of the area is public land administered by a variety of federal and state agencies. These three factors, together with the diverse and broken nature of the terrain, combine to make most of the region a huge de facto wilderness, with endless opportunities for camping.

Regional Highways

The principal approach route to canyon country is the one that defines it on the north, Interstate 70 and U.S. 50. I-70 connects with Denver and Grand Junction to the east, and with U.S. 89 and I-15 to the west. U.S. 6 connects with I-70 just west of the town of Green River and provides an access route from the Salt Lake City vicinity, I-80 and points north.

Access into canyon country from the west can be from I-15 or U.S. 89 via Utah 12 or Utah 24, or via U.S. 89 itself from Kanab to Page. U.S. 160 and Arizona 98 offer access from southern Colorado and points east via U.S. 666 from Cortez to Monticello and U.S. 191. Colorado 90/Utah 46 offers access from the east between I-70 and U.S. 666.

Within canyon country, U.S. 191 and several state highways provide limited access to the various communities and major areas of interest. These are all shown on Utah State highway maps, but may not all appear on multi-state regional highway maps. The canyon country regional map on page 5 of this guidebook shows all canyon country perimeter and access highways, federal and state.

Backcountry Roads and Trails

In addition to the paved regional highways noted, there are many backcountry roads and off-road vehicle trails that provide access to areas otherwise inaccessible for camping or exploring. The roads are either gravel or graded dirt, and may be in poor condition due to flooding, heavy mineral search traffic, infrequent maintenance, or some combination of these factors.

Few backcountry roads appear on Utah State highway maps, but some are shown on regional recreation maps issued by the Utah State Travel Council. Of these, the two covering southeastern Utah show most of the region covered by this guidebook. These maps may be purchased at various visitor centers and retail outlets throughout canyon country.

The general routes of a very few backcountry off-road vehicle trails appear on Utah State highway maps and regional recreation maps, but such information is too limited and inaccurate to be useful.

Five guidebooks and five corresponding maps of the canyon countries describe and illustrate all of the backcountry roads and most of the off-road vehicle trails in the general Moab vicinity. See the pages in the back of this book for titles. Limited information about the backcountry roads and trails in other areas of canyon country can be found on maps issued by the Bureau of Land Management, U.S. Forest Service and National Park Service, as well as on topographic quadrant maps issued by the U.S. Geological Survey.

Hatch Point Campground in the BLM Canyon Rims Recreation Area south of Moab.

Types of Camping

There are four general types of camping available within canyon country: off-highway overnight parking; commercial campgrounds; public campgrounds; and primitive camping.

Off-highway parking is primarily for such self-contained recreation vehicles for motorhomes, pickup-campers, camping vans and trailers that are en route to, from or within canyon country.

Commercial campgrounds are few and widely scattered. Most are within or very near established communities.

Public campgrounds can be found throughout canyon country. Most are within national or state park areas, national forests or special recreation areas.

Primitive camping is defined as any kind of camping at a primitive location, whether undeveloped or only slightly developed, and is available almost anywhere within canyon country except on private land and with certain limitations within some park areas.

Each of the four types of camping listed above is discussed in detail in following chapters of this guidebook. All developed public campgrounds within the region are listed and described in one chapter. Specific sites for all four types of camping are also listed on charts by highway number and special area.

Supplementary Information

For further information on early and recent canyon country explorations; various exploring methods and bases; land, water, and air administration; useful literature; natural history; scenic roads; hiking trails and routes; national and state park areas; river running; off-season travel; traveler facilities, services and supplies; and regional geology and rockhounding, refer to other guidebooks and maps in the Canyon Country series. These are listed in the back of this book. Additional titles in this series are scheduled for release.

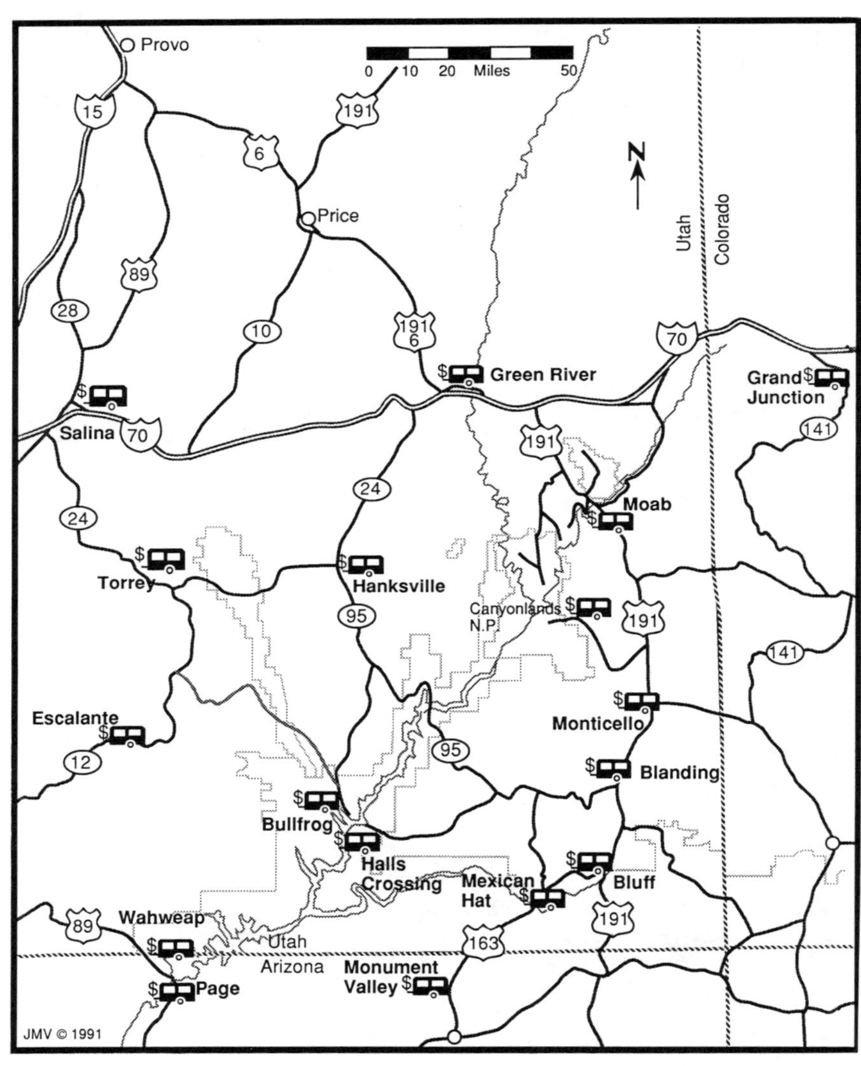

Canyon Country Locations With Commercial Campgrounds.

Commercial Campgrounds

General

There are two types of commercial campgrounds within canyon country: campgrounds that cater strictly to travelers; and mobile home parks that accept overnighters if they have empty spaces. A few such mobile home parks reserve a special section for recreational vehicle use.

Most of the communities within canyon country offer one or both of these types of commercial campgrounds. A few communities, such as Moab and Green River, offer full service, franchise-type commercial campgrounds. Listings of specific commercial campgrounds are not made in this guidebook, because such listings change frequently. This type of information can be found in several different commercial campground directories that are readily available and updated each year.

Seasons

The heaviest travel season in canyon country is mid-May through mid-September, but there is some travel to and through the region year round. Thus, while some traveler-only commercial campgrounds close during the winter months, November through February, others remain open all or most of the winter. Most of the mobile home parks that offer spaces for recreation vehicles remain open year around.

The spring and autumn months in canyon country are generally delightful, neither too hot nor too cold, and the winters are mild to moderate with little or no snow in the lower elevations. Each year, more retirees who travel year around in recreation vehicles are discovering the advantages or wintering in such scenic, low elevation canyon country communities as Moab. As this practice grows, more of the commercial campgrounds that offer full services will remain open year around to accommodate such "seasonal citizens."

Information concerning the open seasons of specific commercial campgrounds can be obtained by writing or calling the campgrounds or the local visitor centers or chambers of commerce, or by consulting campground directories.

Facilities

The facilities offered by canyon country commercial campgrounds vary widely, from poorly maintained spaces with limited hookups and no supporting facilities, to clean, shaded spaces with full hookups and a side range of support facilities and services such as showers, swimming pools, laundries, stores, snack bars, lounges and restrooms. Some even offer reservation services for local guided tours, and a few provide special grassy tent camping sites.

Most of the mobile home parks that offer spaces for travelers provide few if any of the kinds of support facilities and services common to the better traveler-only commercial campgrounds, and most cater only to recreation vehicles.

For a listing of the basic accommodations and support facilities and services offered by various commercial campgrounds within canyon country, write for the literature issued by such campgrounds, or consult any of the various campground directories.

Reservations

In general, reservations are not required or necessary for overnight or short-duration stays at canyon country commercial campgrounds, although as the popularity of this region grows, this may change.

Even now, reservations are advisable for staying at the traveler-only commercial campgrounds located in Moab during the mid-May through mid-September travel season, and especially over the Easter, Memorial Day, Independence Day and Labor Day weekends. This may apply to the campgrounds in other communities too, as travel into and through the region increases.

Travelers who wish to stay in commercial campgrounds within the more popular areas of canyon country for more than a few days, whatever the season, are advised to make space reservations well in advance in order to avoid disappointment. This is especially true for motorhome or trailer owners who travel in groups.

Canyon country visitors planning to take longer tours through the region, such as one of the "circle routes," should definitely make reservations at each planned stop along their route, well in advance of the trip, and should allow for plenty of time at each stop.

Locations

Specific locations of commercial campgrounds are not given in this guidebook, because this kind of information is subject to change, but general locations are given in the highway camping charts later in this book. The addresses for individual campgrounds can be obtained in advance from campground directories, or by writing to local visitor centers or chambers of commerce.

Travelers who arrive in a canyon country community without advance knowledge of commercial campground locations can inquire at local visitor centers, service stations or other commercial establishments, but should be aware that commercial business employees in this region are often poorly informed about traveler accommodations.

In general, most traveler-only commercial campgrounds are on or near the highways that serve various communities, and have conspicuous signs indicating their locations. Mobile home parks that offer overnight spaces may be similarly located, but more often are on side streets or roads and may not have signs within sight of the main highways.

The entrance to Green River State Park, one of canyon country's many developed public campgrounds.

Public Campgrounds

General

There are quite a few public campgrounds within canyon country, but the region is so large that these campgrounds are widely scattered. Further, most of them are located too far from the main highways for practical overnight use. Thus, it is generally worth the effort to reach a public campground only if more than one night is going to be spent in the area.

Most public campgrounds in canyon country are administered either by the State of Utah or by one of three federal agencies, the National Park Service, the U.S. Forest Service on the Bureau of Land Management. Thus, most are located within special areas having high scenic and recreational value.

A few of the public campgrounds, such as those in national park areas, are regularly patrolled by rangers, but most other parks are visited only occasionally by maintenance personnel or rangers.

Seasons

The open seasons for public campgrounds in canyon country will vary, depending upon elevation, accessibility, visitation records and administrative policies. Some campgrounds, such as those in the mountains, are closed by the first autumn snows and do not re-open until late spring. Some at lower elevations may remain open, but their water is shut off during the colder months to avoid damage from freezing. Others are open year around, but offer no water and few developed facilities. Rarely are any of the public campgrounds in this region closed, with access physically barred, at any season. In general no matter what the season or weather, if the campground can be reached, it can be used.

Facilities

The facilities in various canyon country public campgrounds range from a few tables, a pit toilet and nothing more, to elaborate sites and ramadas, slabs, water and electrical hookups. The general level of facility development at each public campground is listed later in this chapter, but changes can be expected as campgrounds are improved.

It should be noted that not all public campgrounds in the more arid areas of canyon country provide water. Because of this, campers should always be prepared to supply their own water, unless they know in advance that water is available at their destination campground. In the cooler months, even campgrounds that normally provide water may have their pipes drained to prevent freezing.

Although there may be retail sources of supplies reasonably close to a few public campgrounds, most are quite distant from camping provisions. It is thus necessary, for those planning to use canyon country public campgrounds, to take with them enough food and other supplies to last for the duration of their stay.

In most cases, especially within national park areas, campers must also bring with them any firewood they may choose to use for cooking or campfires. Collecting wood in national parks and monuments is not permitted. Driftwood collection and burning in national recreation areas is permissible, except where otherwise posted.

A few of the larger public campgrounds, such as those in national park areas, provide facilities for dumping recreation vehicle sanitary hold tanks, but most do not. Owners of such vehicles planning to visit public campgrounds are advised to empty their hold tanks at service stations, trailer parks or other dump stations before reaching the campgrounds.

Reservations

None of the public campgrounds in canyon country are operated on a reservation system. Sites are filled on a first-come, first-served basis, with occupancy time limits applicable to some campgrounds during the main travel season. Some of the campgrounds in national park areas may have occupancy time limits year around. A few public campgrounds make reservations for the use of their special group areas.

With some campgrounds, such as those within national park areas, it is possible to check on site availability, at either visitor centers or entrance stations, before driving to the campground. Generally, if the campgrounds in the more popular park service areas are full, some type of overflow, one-night parking is provided.

Most of the public campgrounds in the region charge overnight fees. Both state and federally administered campgrounds accept the appropriate seasonal passes in lieu of park or all of the overnight fee, but Utah State park passes are honored only in Utah State administered campgrounds, and federal passes are honored only in campgrounds administered by federal agencies. In some fee campgrounds, the fees are collected on an honor system. In others the fees are collected by rangers each evening.

Locations

In general, the locations of canyon country public campgrounds are related to public administration. There are Utah State Park campgrounds within state park areas, National Park Service campgrounds with the region's several national parks, monuments and recreation areas, U.S. Forest Service campgrounds within the national forests, and Bureau of Land Management campgrounds in areas administered by that agency.

Specific locations of all the public campgrounds in canyon country appear with the following campground descriptions, and also appear on the highway camping charts and special area charts that appear later in this guidebook.

Index to Public Campgrounds

1. Buckboard
2. Buckeye
3. Bullfrog
4. Capitol Reef
5. Dalton Springs
6. Deadhorse Point
7. Devils Canyon
8. Devils Garden
9. Goblin Valley
10. Goosenecks
11. Green River
12. Halls Crossing
13. Hatch Point
14. Hite
15. Hovenweep
16. Lees Ferry
17. Lonesome Bever
18. McMillan Springs
19. Natural Bridges
20. Newspaper Rock
21. Oowah Lake
22. Red Bluff
23. Sand Island
24. Squaw Flat
25. Starr Springs
26. Wahweep
27. Warner Lake
28. Willow Flat
29. Windwhistle

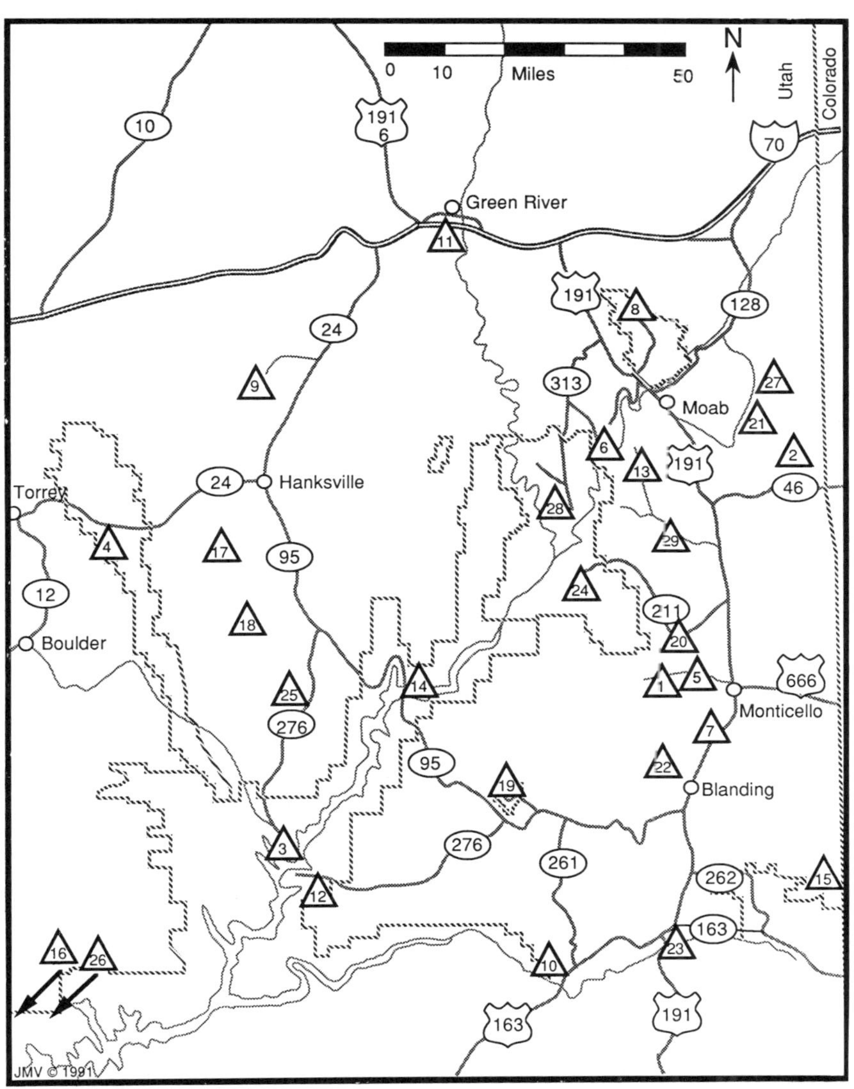

Locations Of Public Campgrounds

Description Format

The following standardized format is followed in describing the public campgrounds in canyon country. All data is subject to change, but such changes will generally be for the better. Campgrounds are listed alphabetically.

It should be noted by travelers approaching canyon country from southwestern Utah or southwestern Colorado that there are quite a few national forest campgrounds just outside of the canyon country region. These are not described in the guidebook, but can be found listed in travel literature issued by Utah, Colorado and the U.S. Forest Service. Public campgrounds near various approach routes, but not within canyon country, are also not described, but may be noted in the highway camping charts elsewhere in this guidebook if they are within practical overnight range of the highway.

Name. The official campground name assigned by the administering agency is given. If the campground has no name, it is named after the special area in which it is located.

Location. The general location, such as in a park or some other special area, is given, together with the number of the nearest federal or state highway.

Access. The type and quality of road between the nearest paved highway and the campground is noted, together with the approximate distance from the highway.

Sites. The number of sites is listed, indicating the size of the campground. This number should be considered only approximate. If the campground has a special group area, this is noted.

Facilities. Standard campground facilities are listed, such as water, tables, grills, toilets, ramadas, hookups and dump stations.

Elevation. Campground elevations above sea level are listed, as a guide to climate and for travelers sensitive to high elevations.

Season. The official open season of each campground is listed, but actual open seasons may vary each year.

Setting. A brief description of the campground setting is given as an aid to campground selection.

Fee. Whether or not a use fee is usually charged is noted, but this can be expected to vary seasonally.

Supplies. The nearest sources of camping supplies are noted.

Recreation. General types of recreation available from the campground are noted.

Directions. Detailed directions for reaching the campground from the nearest federal or state highway are given. Back country road and trail nomenclature in the general Moab vicinity is standardized in the six off-road vehicle trail guidebooks and maps listed in the back of this book.

Comments. Any hints or personal observations by guidebook author are listed here.

Descriptions

Buckboard

Location: Abajo Mountains; U.S. 191
Access: 5 miles of paved road, 1 mile of graded dirt, from U.S. 191
Sites: 10; Group area
Facilities: Water, tables, grills, toilets
Elevation: 8600 feet
Season: July through October
Setting: Mountains, forested
Fee: Yes
Supplies: Monticello, 6 miles
Recreation: Hiking, hunting in season, off-road vehicle exploring in vicinity
Directions: Drive due west from center of Monticello, past Dalton Springs Campground, follow signs to Buckboard Campground
Comments: Suggest non-hunters avoid this and other mountain campgrounds during the Utah deer hunting season

Buckeye

Location: La Sal Mountains; Utah 46 or Colorado 90
Access: Graded dirt road; 18 miles from Utah 46
Sites: 8; group area
Facilities: Tables, grills, toilets; no water
Elevation: 7600 feet
Season: May through October
Setting: Mountain lake, forested
Fee: No
Supplies: La Sal, 23 miles
Recreation: Hiking, swimming, boating, fishing, hunting in season, off-road vehicle exploring in vicinity
Directions: Drive north from Utah 46 on Canopy Gap Road to where it ends, then east on Geyser Pass trail to Buckeye Reservoir; alternatively, drive from Colorado 90 to Paradox, then take Paradox-Buckeye Road to Buckeye Reservoir
Comments: Lovely setting, but accessible to highway-type vehicles only when road is dry

Bullfrog

Location: Bullfrog Basin, Lake Powell; Utah 276
Access: Paved road; 1/4 mile from Utah 276
Sites: 86
Facilities: Water, tables, grills toilets, dump station
Elevation: 4000 feet
Season: Year around
Setting: Open desert
Fee: Yes
Supplies: Bullfrog Marina, 1 Mile
Recreation: Hiking, boating, fishing, water sports, swimming nearby, off-road vehicle exploring in vicinity
Directions: Campground is beside Utah 276 at the Bullfrog developed area
Comments: No shade; very hot, dry and windy during spring and summer months; launch ramp and boat rentals at nearby marina

Capitol Reef

Location: Capitol Reef National Park; Utah 24
Access: Paved road; 1 1/2 miles from Utah 24
Sites: 53
Facilities: Water, tables, grills, toilets
Elevation: 5200 feet
Season: Year around
Setting: Wooded valley
Fee: Yes
Supplies: Torrey, 12 miles west; Hanksville, 44 miles east
Recreation: Hiking, sightseeing, off-road vehicle exploring in vicinity
Directions: Campground is near Utah 24 in the main developed area within the park; follow signs from highway
Comments: Lovely setting; generally full during the summer travel season

Dalton Springs

Location: Abajo Mountains, U.S. 191
Access: Paved road; 5 miles from U.S. 191
Sites: 14
Facilities: Water, tables, grills, toilets
Elevation: 8200 feet
Season: July through October
Setting: Mountains, forested
Fee: No
Supplies: Monticello, 5 miles
Recreation: Hiking, hunting in season, off-road vehicle exploration in vicinity
Directions: Drive due west from center of Monticello on paved road
Comments: Suggest non-hunters avoid this and other mountain campgrounds during Utah deer hunting season

Dead Horse Point

Location: Dead Horse Point State Park; Utah 313
Access: Paved road, 1/4 mile from Utah 313
Sites: 21; group areas
Facilities: Water, tables, grills, toilets, ramadas, electrical hookups, dump station
Elevation: 5900 feet
Season: Year around
Setting: Plateau top, pinyon-juniper woods
Fee: Yes
Supplies: Moab, 33 miles
Recreation: Hiking, sightseeing, off-road vehicle exploring outside of park
Directions: Drive west on Utah 313 from U.S. 191; campground is within park, near end of paved road
Comments: Excellent campground in a spectacular setting; use water sparingly, it is all trucked in from Moab; nearby visitor center and museum; short, steep grade about 3 miles from U.S. 191.

Rim Overlook at Deadhorse Point State Park

Devils Canyon

Location: Abajo Mountains, U.S. 191
Access: Paved road; 1/2 mile from U.S. 191
Sites: 33; group area
Facilities: Water, tables, grills, toilets
Elevation: 7100 feet
Season: May through October
Setting: Wooded canyon rim
Fee: Yes
Supplies: Monticello, 11 miles north; Blanding, 12 miles south
Recreation: Hiking, hunting in season, off-road vehicle exploring in vicinity
Directions: Campground is very near Highway, about midway between Monticello and Blanding, just south of highway dip into Devil's Canyon
Comments: Shaded sites, an excellent overnight stop close to a main travel route; suggest non-hunters avoid this and other mountain campgrounds during the Utah deer hunting season

Devils Garden

Location: Arches National Park; U.S. 191
Access: Paved road; 17 miles from U.S. 191
Sites: 53; group area
Facilities: Water, tables, grills, toilets
Elevation: 5300 feet
Season: Year around
Setting: Redrock desert, pinyon-juniper woods
Fee: Yes
Supplies: Moab, 22 miles
Recreation: Hiking, sightseeing, off-road vehicle exploring within park and in vicinity
Directions: Drive into the park to the end of the paved road in the Devils Garden area; campground is on a short spur road
Comments: Limited shade; setting is very picturesque; excellent hiking, sightseeing in the vicinity

Escalante Petrified Forest State Park

Location: Near the town of Escalante
Access: Graded road, 1/2 mile from Utah 12
Sites: 21
Facilities: Water, tables, grills, toilets, showers
Elevation: 5800 feet
Season: Year around
Setting: Open area below pinyon-juniper forest
Fee: Yes
Supplies: Escalante, 1-1/2 miles east
Recreation: Hiking into nearby petrified forest
Directions: Drive about 1 mile west from Escalante on Utah 12, then 1/2 mile north on a graded road into the park

Goblin Valley

Location: Goblin Valley State Park; Utah 24
Access: 5-1/2 miles of paved road, 6-1/2 miles of graded dirt road from Utah 24
Sites: 20
Facilities: Water, tables, toilets, dump station
Elevation: 5200 feet
Season: Year around
Setting: Among picturesque desert rock formations
Fee: Yes
Supplies: Hanksville, 32 miles south; Green River, 49 miles north
Recreation: Hiking, sightseeing, off-road vehicle exploring outside of park
Directions: Turn west from Utah 24 on paved road about 25 miles south of I-70; after 5-1/2 miles, turn south on graded dirt road; campground is beside road in park development area
Comments: Campground setting very picturesque; no shade; very dusty when windy.

Goosenecks

Location: Goosenecks of the San Juan State Reserve; Utah 261
Access: Paved road; 3-1/2 miles from Utah 261
Sites: 6
Facilities: Tables, toilets; no water
Elevation: 4500 feet
Season: Year around
Setting: Canyon rim, open desert
Fee: No
Supplies: Mexican Hat, 7 miles
Recreation: Hiking, sightseeing, off-road vehicle exploring in vicinity
Directions: Drive north on Utah 261 from U.S. 191 for about 1 mile, then west on paved road (Utah 316) for 3-1/2 miles; campground is at end of road
Comments: Spectacular view from rim near campground; no shade; very dusty when windy; convenient overnight stop for recreation vehicles near a main travel route

Green River

Location: Green River State Recreational Area; I-70 & U.S. 50
Access: Paved road; 1/2 mile from I-70 & U.S. 50
Sites: 40, group area
Facilities: Water, tables, grills, toilets, showers, boat launch ramp
Elevation: 4100 feet
Season: Year around
Setting: Riverbank trees
Fee: Yes
Supplies: Green River, 1/2 mile
Recreation: River boating, fishing, swimming, off-road vehicle exploring outside of park
Directions: Just east of Green River town center, turn south and follow signs to park and campground; both are on the west side of the Green River
Comments: Shaded sites; boat launch ramp is commonly used by river runners using rubber rafts, but is useful to conventional boats only during brief high water periods; river currents make swimming hazardous.

Houseboating on Lake Powell

Halls Crossing

Location: Halls Crossing, Lake Powell; Utah 263
Access: Paved road; 1/4 mile from Utah 263
Sites: 30
Facilities: Water, tables, grills, toilet
Elevation: 4000 feet
Season: Year around
Setting: Open desert
Fee: Yes
Supplies: Halls Crossing Marina, 1/2 mile
Recreation: Hiking, boating, fishing, water sports, swimming nearby, off-road vehicle exploring in vicinity
Directions: Campground is beside Utah 263 at the Halls Crossing developed area
Comments: No shade; very hot, dry and windy during spring and summer months; launch ramp and boat rentals at nearby marina

Hatch Point

Location: Canyon Rims Recreation Area; U.S. 191
Access: Paved road, 15 miles, gravel road 10 miles; from U.S. 191
Sites: 10
Facilities: Water, tables, grills, toilets
Elevation: 5800 feet
Season: Year around
Setting: Bluff-rim, pinyon-juniper woods
Fee: No
Supplies: Moab, 58 miles north,; Monticello, 45 miles south
Recreation: Hiking, sightseeing, off-road vehicle exploring in vicinity
Directions: Drive west 15 miles on paved road that leaves U.S. 191 about 34 miles south of Moab, then north about 9 miles on gravel road; campground is 1 mile east of main gravel road and indicated by a sign
Comments: Campground is lightly used; setting is picturesque; some shade; antelope sometimes seen nearby

Hite

Location: Hite, Lake Powell; Utah 95
Access: Paved road; 2 miles from Utah 95
Sites: No developed sites
Facilities: No developed facilities
Elevation: 3800 feet
Season: Year around
Setting: Redrock desert, lakeshore
Fee: No
Supplies: Hite Marina, 1 mile
Recreation: Hiking, boating, fishing, swimming, water sports, off-road vehicle exploring in vicinity
Directions: About 1 mile south of the Utah 95 bridge over Lake Powell, turn west on paved road toward Hite developed area; campground is beside road about 2 miles from Utah 95
Comments: Designated camping areas; no shade, but very picturesque setting; very hot, dry and windy during spring and summer months; launch ramp and boat rentals at nearby marina.

Hovenweep

Location: Hovenweep National Monument; Utah 262
Access: Graded dirt road; 16 miles from Utah 262
Sites: 31
Facilities: Water, tables, grills, ramadas, toilets
Elevation: 5200 feet
Season: Year around
Setting: Open pinyon-juniper woods
Fee: Yes
Supplies: Blanding, 31 miles; Bluff, 27 miles
Recreation: Hiking, sightseeing, off-road vehicle exploring outside of monument
Directions: Drive east from U.S. 191 on Utah 262 for 8-1/2 miles, then continue east on graded dirt road for about 15 miles; follow signs to campground near monument headquarters
Comments: Little shade; very hot during summer months; biting insects during certain seasons

Ruins at Hovenweep National Monument

Lees Ferry

Location: Glen Canyon National Recreation Area; U.S. 89A
Access: Paved road; 6 miles from U.S. 89A
Sites: 56
Facilities: Water, tables, grills, toilets, ramadas
Elevation: 3200 feet
Season: Year around
Setting: River gorge; beside Colorado River
Fee: Yes
Supplies: Camp store nearby
Recreation: Hiking, fishing, boating, off-road vehicle exploring in vicinity
Directions: Turn north from U.S. 89A on paved road at Marble Junction, where highway crosses Colorado River gorge; follow signs on paved road to Lees Ferry and campground
Comments: Lees Ferry is the principal launch point for running the Colorado River through the Grand Canyon; very hot during summer months

Lonesome Beaver

Location: Henry Mountains: Utah 95
Access: Graded dirt road; 21 miles from Utah 24
Sites: 7; group area
Facilities: Water, tables, grills, toilets
Elevation: 8200 feet
Season: June through November
Setting: Mountains, forested
Fee: No
Supplies: Hanksville, 21 miles
Recreation: Hiking, hunting in season, rockhounding and offroad vehicle exploring in vicinity
Directions: Drive south from Hanksville on Sawmill Basin Road into Henry Mountains; campground is beside road, about 21 miles from Hanksville; road east from Utah 95 about 10-1/2 miles south of Hanksville joins Sawmill Basin Road after about 6 miles
Comments: Access road steep and rough in mountains; not recommended for standard highway vehicles; not accessible to large recreation vehicles

McMillan Springs

Location: Henry Mountains; Utah 24 or Utah 95
Access: Graded dirt roads; 37 miles from Utah 24, 24 miles from Utah 95
Sites: 10
Facilities: Tables, grills, toilets; no water
Elevation: 8350 feet
Season: June through November
Setting: Mountains, forested
Fee: No
Supplies: Hanksville, 58 miles via Notom and Utah 24
Recreation: Hiking, hunting in season, rockhounding and off-road vehicle exploring in vicinity
Directions: About 21 miles west of Hanksville on U24, drive about 17 miles south on Notom-Bullfrog Road, turn east on Blind Trail toward King Ranch and Nasty Flat; campground is about 20 miles from Notom-Bullfrog Road; from U24 or U95, go to Lonesome Beaver Campground, then continue southwest on mountain roads for about 10 miles to McMillan Springs Campground
Comments: Access roads steep and rough in mountains; not recommended for standard highway vehicles; not accessible to large recreation vehicles; U.S.G.S. topo maps call the spring near this campground "McLellan Spring"

Natural Bridges

Location: Natural Bridges National Monument; Utah 95
Access: Paved road; 5 miles from Utah 95
Sites: 13
Facilities: Water, tables, grills, toilets
Elevation: 6500 feet
Season: Year around
Setting: Dense pinyon-juniper woods
Fee: Yes
Supplies: Blanding, 38 miles east; Hite, 52 miles northwest
Recreation: Hiking, sightseeing, off-road vehicle exploring outside of monument
Directions: About 2 miles west of the U95/U261 junction on Utah 95, turn north on paved road into monument developed area; follow signs to campground
Comments: Nearby visitor center

Newspaper Rock

Location: Newspaper Rock State Historical Monument; Utah 211
Access: Beside paved highway
Sites: 9
Facilities: Tables, toilets; no potable water
Elevation: 6150 feet
Season: Year Around
Setting: Canyon-stream woods
Fee: No
Supplies: Monticello, 27 miles
Recreation: Hiking, sightseeing, off-road vehicle exploring in vicinity
Directions: Campground is beside Utah 211 about 12 miles west of U.S. 191 and across the highway from Newspaper Rock
Comments: Lovely, canyon-bottom setting; convenient and interesting overnight stop beside highway into Needles District of Canyonlands National Park; purify stream water before using

Oowah Lake

Location: La Sal Mountains; U.S. 191
Access: Paved road, 5 1/2 miles; rough, steep dirt road, 11 miles, from U.S. 191
Sites: 13
Facilities: Water, tables, grills, toilets
Elevation: 8800 feet
Season: June through October
Setting: Mountains, lake and stream, forested
Fee: Yes
Supplies: Moab, 25 miles
Recreation: Hiking, fishing, boating, swimming, hunting in season, off-road vehicle exploring in vicinity
Directions: Drive southeast from Moab on Spanish Valley Road; at Pack Creek junction, take graded dirt Loop Road; after about 8 miles, turn right and drive about 3 miles to Oowah Lake; campground is at end of road near lake.
Comments: Lovely mountain setting; accessible to standard highway vehicles only when road is dry; accessible only to small recreation vehicles; alternate, longer but mostly paved approach is via Utah 128, Castle Valley, northern end of Loop Road; suggest non-hunters avoid during Utah deer hunting season

Red Bluff

Location: Abajo Mountains; U.S. 191
Access: Paved and dirt road; 14 miles from U.S. 191
Sites: 5
Facilities: Tables, grills, toilets; no water
Elevation: 8200 feet
Season: June through October
Setting: Mountains, forested
Fee: No
Supplies: Blanding, 14 miles
Recreation: Hiking, hunting in season, off-road vehicle exploring in vicinity
Directions: Drive north out of Blanding, stay on Forest Service Road #079 and follow signs to campground
Comments: U.S. Forest Service maps of Manti-La Sal National Forest show the roads in the Abajo Mountains

Sand Island

Location: Near San Juan River; U.S. 191
Access: Short gravel road from U.S. 191
Sites: 6
Facilities: Tables, grills, toilets; no potable water
Elevation: 4300 feet
Season: Year around
Setting: Desert, riverbank trees
Fee: No
Supplies: Bluff, 4 miles
Recreation: Hiking, sightseeing, off-road vehicle exploring in vicinity
Directions: Drive 3-1/2 miles west of Bluff on U.S. 191; turn south at sign and take dirt road to campground
Comments: Several archaeological sites nearby; launch site for river runners; do not use river for culinary purposes

Squaw Flat

Location: Needles District, Canyonlands National Park; Utah 211
Access: Paved road from end of Utah 211
Sites: 27; group area
Facilities: Water, tables, grills, toilets
Elevation: 5100 feet
Season: Year around
Setting: Redrock desert, pinyon-juniper woods
Fee: Yes
Supplies: Canyonlands Resort, 4 miles (when open); Monticello, 52 miles
Recreation: Hiking, sightseeing, off-road vehicle exploring within park and in vicinity
Directions: Drive to west end of Utah 211 and continue on paved road into park; follow signs to campground
Comments: Exceptionally beautiful and unusual setting; easy access to many highly scenic hiking and off-road vehicle trails

Squaw Flat Campground, Needles District, Canyonlands National Park

Starr Springs

Location: Henry Mountains, Utah 276
Access: Graded dirt road; 3-1/2 miles from Utah 276
Sites: 12
Facilities: Water, tables, grills, toilets
Elevation: 6160 feet
Season: April through November
Setting: Mountain stream, wooded
Fee: No
Supplies: Bullfrog Marina, 27 miles south, Hite Marina, 45 miles east; Hanksville, 50 miles north
Recreation: Hiking, sightseeing, hunting in season, rockhounding and off-road vehicle exploring in vicinity
Directions: About 18 miles from Utah 95, turn north from Utah 276 onto dirt road indicated by Starr Springs sign; drive about 3-1/2 miles to campground
Comments: Historic Starr Ranch is near campground; accessible to standard highway vehicles only when road is dry; not accessible to large recreation vehicles because of rough road and steep grades

Wahweap

Location: Wahweap Bay, Lake Powell; U.S. 89
Access: Paved road; 3 miles from U.S. 89
Sites: 179; group area
Facilities: Water, tables, grills, toilets, dump station
Elevation: 3800 feet
Season: Year around
Setting: Open desert
Fee: Yes
Supplies: Wahweap Marina, 1 mile; Page, 8 miles
Recreation: Hiking, boating, fishing, water sports, swimming nearby, off-road vehicle exploring in vicinity
Directions: Follow signs from Glen Canyon Dam visitor center, or leave U.S. 89 about 6 miles northwest of Page and follow signs to campground
Comments: Little shade, very hot, dry and windy during spring and summer months; launch ramp and boat rentals at nearby marina; visitor center and museum nearby at dam

Warner Lake

Location: La Sal Mountains; Utah 128
Access: Paved road, 20 miles; graded dirt road, 5 miles, from Utah 128
Sites: 20; group area
Facilities: Water, tables, grills, toilets
Elevation: 9200 feet
Season: June through October
Setting: Mountains, lake, forested
Fee: Yes
Supplies: Moab, 43 miles
Recreation: Hiking, fishing, hunting in season, off-road vehicle exploring in vicinity

Directions: Turn onto paved Castle Valley Road from Utah 128 about 15 miles from U.S. 191, turn onto paved end of Loop Road at sign in upper Castle Valley; in about 11 miles, turn onto graded dirt Warner Lake Road at sign; campground is at end of road, beside lake
Comments: Picturesque aspen forest setting, with wild flowers all summer, brilliant colors in autumn; lake is too shallow for swimming, too small for boating; last 5 miles passable to standard highway vehicles only when dirt road is dry; accessible only to small recreation vehicles because of steep grades

Warner Lake in the La Sal Mountains

Willow Flat

Location: Island in the Sky District, Canyonlands National Park; Utah 313
Access: Graded dirt road; 15 miles from Utah 313
Sites: 8
Facilities: Tables, grills, toilets; no water
Elevation: 6200 feet
Season: Year around
Setting: Mesa top, pinyon-juniper woods
Fee: No
Supplies: Moab, 42 miles
Recreation: Hiking, sightseeing, off-road vehicle exploring within park and in vicinity
Directions: Leave Utah 313 at the Knoll Junction, about 15 miles from U.S. 191, continue south on graded dirt Island Road; follow signs to Green River Overlook; campground is beside road just before overlook
Comments: Shade limited; spectacular mesa-rim overlook near campground; dirt road passable to standard highway vehicles only when dry; part of access road scheduled for improvement

Wind Whistle

Location: Canyon Rims Recreation Area; U.S. 191
Access: Paved road; 6 miles from U.S. 191
Sites: 19
Facilities: Water, tables, grills, toilets
Elevation: 6000 feet
Season: Year around
Setting: Redrock desert, pinyon-juniper woods
Fee: Yes
Supplies: Moab, 40 miles
Recreation: Hiking, sightseeing, off-road vehicle exploring in vicinity
Directions: Drive west 6 miles on paved road that leaves U.S. 191 about 12 miles south of La Sal Junction; campground is beside road
Comments: Beautiful setting; convenient location for visiting the major overlooks in this recreation area, and for an overnight stop close to a main travel route; roomy sites

Off-highway parking near highway US191

Off-Highway Overnight Parking

General

Overnight camping or vehicle parking are permitted almost anywhere on public land beyond the highway right-of-way. Off-highway overnight parking is commonly used as an informal stopover en route to a destination in canyon country. The main restriction is that overnight camping and parking is prohibited by Utah law at developed highway or freeway rest stops, at scenic pull-outs or on the highway right-of-way anywhere. Also, off-highway parking is not allowed on the Navajo Indian Reservation. In practice, this means no parking along the shoulder of paved roads or south of the San Juan river.

Suitable campsites may be found on unusually wide pull-outs beside a highway, or on open or graded ground a short distance from the highway beside a spur road. When looking for a campsite, watch for small and often inconspicuous roads that branch from the main roads. Many such spur roads have been created over the years by mining exploration and ranching activities. Some go only a short way before becoming too rough for standard highway vehicles, so drive carefully.

There may be gates across some such spur roads. Most of the land in canyon country is public land that is leased for grazing and the fences and gates are to control livestock and not to exclude people. If the land beyond the gate seems to be developed in anyway, or is posted, it is probably private land and should not be entered. However, if the land beyond the gate is open scrub brush or grassland and if the only sign says "Please Close The Gate" the land beyond the gate can be assumed to be public, with overnight camping and parking permitted.

The gate should be closed after each use. The most common gate consists of three strands of barbed wire with short spacers and with a stout pole on the end. It is secured to the fence post at one end with two loops of wire. The trick to closing one of these gates without cutting your hand is to place the lower end of the stout pole in the loop of wire near the ground first. Then use the pole as a lever to pull the gate tight, and finally swing the upper loop of wire down over the top of the pole.

Locations

Off-highway overnight parking can be found beside or near every federal or state highway in canyon country, although along some, such as where I-70 and U.S. 50 are completed freeway, legal overnight parking can only be found by leaving the freeway on a side road.

Some suggested off-highway overnight parking sites are listed in the highway camping charts later in this guidebook.

There are several things to watch for when looking for a suitable site for overnight parking. For safety, get well off the main road. Watch for spur roads where vegetation or rolling terrain will give a little screening from the noise and headlights on the highway. Often, driving a hundred yards to half a mile along a spur road will lead to a pullout created by previous camping use, a turnaround near a water trough or corral, or just an open and level area.

If camping inside a vehicle, the only remaining concern is to get off to one side in case someone else wants to drive by during the night.

Rain and insects are not a problem for most of the year, and many visitors to canyon country simply throw their sleeping bags on the ground beside their vehicle when parking overnight. The idea is to find a level spot, free of brush and cactus. Sometimes the best sleeping bag spot is right beside the car, especially if arriving late. In this case, be sure you are not sleeping in the travel path of any vehicles that come through at night. But usually, walking a few feet from the spur road will be worth the effort.

Campsite Manners

When camping at an off-highway parking spot use common sense and common courtesy. Pick your site with care and avoid creating any hazard or nuisance. Since these sites are undeveloped and unmaintained, use low-impact camping techniques and clean up your mess before leaving.

On popular weekends in spring and fall the best off-highway sites may have several vehicles using the spot. This is especially true on Friday nights when a lot of city-dwellers are traveling to southern Utah. Park carefully to leave room for others. If arriving late, minimize noise and headlights.

If practical, try to disperse the use to allow others some space and to avoid creating site damage or sanitation problems.

Primitive camping in the mountains that rise above canyon country.

Primitive Camping

General

Because over 90 percent of the area of canyon country is public land, there are almost endless opportunities there for primitive camping. This public land is administered by one or the other of four agencies: Utah State, the National Park Service, the U.S. Forest Service or the Bureau of Land Management. The Navajo Indian reservation to the south of the canyon country region is administered by the Navajo tribe and the Bureau of Indian Affairs.

Some of the state land has been consolidated into larger areas and is leased for special purposes. A few special areas have been set aside as state parks, recreation areas, historic monuments or reserves. Other state land is in the form of isolated sections scattered all over the state. A section is one square mile in size.

Leased state lands are generally closed to uses other than those indicated in the leases, such as mining or agriculture. Within state park areas, camping is usually restricted to designated sites which precludes primitive camping. The scattered sections of state land are usually not marked or indicated in any way, and are administered for multiple use. Therefore, primitive camping is permitted on them unless posted otherwise.

Within most National Park Service areas, primitive camping from vehicles is generally restricted to certain designated sites in order to minimize damage to the park terrain. For backpackers, primitive camping is less restricted. Within the Glen Canyon National Recreation Area, primitive camping from land vehicles or boats is restricted only within the developed areas near the marinas. camping is not permitted within Rainbow Bridge National Monument.

In general, primitive camping is permitted anywhere on National Forest Land, except in the vicinity of certain campgrounds and lakes where posted, and except during exceptionally dry periods when the fire hazard is high.

On land administered by the Bureau of Land Management, primitive camping is permitted anywhere except in the vicinity of developed campgrounds, or where otherwise posted.

For further details on public land administration in canyon country, see "Canyon Country Exploring."

Types

Within canyon country, there are three general types of primitive camping: on land, from a vehicle or backpack; along rivers, from a vehicle or boat; and on Lake Powell, from a vehicle or boat. Since variables, such as seasons, access, site selection, and problems and hazards, will differ with each type, the following discussions consider these differences.

Seasons

In general, the season for primitive camping in canyon country will vary with the climate, the prevailing weather, the elevation and personal equipment and inclination.

Those with self-contained vehicles who do not mind weather and temperature extremes will enjoy primitive camping in canyon country year around, with plenty of beautiful sites accessible no matter what the season.

Tent-campers, or those without heated recreation vehicles, will find the winter season, usually from December through February, too cold for primitive camping.

Vehicle or backpack campers who simply throw bedrolls on the ground will generally find the April through October season warm enough, but sometimes unusual weather creates exceptions to this.

Boat campers, on Lake Powell or along the rivers, will find the April through October season best, with the exceptions noted. Lake Powell boaters using heated, self-contained houseboats or cabin cruisers will be able to enjoy shoreline camping year around, although they may encounter special problems from the low temperatures during the winter, December through February. Winter boating of any kind on canyon country rivers is generally not practical because of low water, low temperatures and ice.

Canyon country weather can sometimes make primitive camping less enjoyable. Although the general climate is arid, major storms do occasionally reach the region, sometimes causing heavy rains and strong winds. Wind is also common at other times, particularly in the spring, or associated with summer thunderhead cloud systems.

Most rain is generally of short duration. Even major storms rarely bring threat of precipitation for longer than a day or two. Winds associated with major storms generally precede the storms by a day or so, and linger following the storm. Winds associated with thunderhead cloud systems are often strong, but of short duration. Wind associated with major seasonal changes, such as Winter-to-Spring, may blow steadily for days, but with the weather otherwise good.

Winds of moderate velocity are usually no hazard to primitive camping, even types of camping that are more exposed to the elements, because by its nature the desert soil of canyon country is held firmly against moderate wind and water erosion, and dust during such wind is minimal. An exception to this is where human activity has damaged or destroyed the soil's protective crust. In such places, even mild winds can pick up dust and sand and make camping in the open very unpleasant. Similarly, camping near "living sand dune" areas, where the sand is not held by a natural crust, can be unpleasant when winds blow. Canyon country has few large "living dune" areas, but many smaller ones.

Elevation can also affect primitive camping, principally by shortening the practical camping season at higher elevations. Although snowfall varies widely within canyon country from year to year, some snow generally falls above 6000 feet in

December and lasts through February. Above 7000 feet, the snow season may be from November through March or April, with all vehicle access blocked for that period. Above 8000 feet, the snow season may extend into May or June, although it may not start before October, November or even December.

Although vehicle access is blocked by snow in the higher elevations during the winter, those who enjoy and are equipped for snowshoe backpacking or cross-country skiing will find canyon country higher elevations both accessible and delightful.

Access

With the exceptions noted earlier, canyon country is open to primitive camping almost anywhere that it is possible to reach by land vehicle, boat or on foot. Access to primitive camping sites is thus by highway, road, off-road vehicle trail, river, lake or hiking trail or route.

Other canyon country guidebooks and maps describe many of these access routes in detail. See the listing in the back of this book. Various state highway and general recreation maps show the main regional highways.

In general, access into canyon country for purposes of primitive camping from standard highway vehicles and larger recreation vehicles is limited to paved roads, plus the better graded dirt roads described in this and other canyon country guidebooks. Various types of off-road vehicles can penetrate more deeply into the canyon country hinterlands, and thus provide still more opportunities for primitive camping. Backpacking, river running and lake-boating open up still other vast areas of terrain not accessible to any type of land vehicle. In these areas, primitive camping is essential, because of the wilderness nature of the backcountry.

Site Selection

Site selection for primitive camping in canyon country will depend upon the type of camping equipment being used, and such variables as the terrain, weather, local hazards, the need for firewood, and amount of nearby scenic beauty desired.

In general, sites near lakes, rivers, streams, canyon or mesa rims, scenic overlooks or in wooded areas are excellent, although there may be hazards associated with such sites. During the warmer months, shade is important. In the cooler months, firewood availability is a prime consideration.

For campers with such recreation vehicles as motorhomes, large trailers or large campers, primitive camping is generally limited to off-highway parking as discussed earlier, although with care some of the graded dirt backcountry roads in canyon country can be traveled by such vehicles.

Small recreation vehicles that are powered by two wheel drive will largely be restricted to off-highway, off-road parking, but will be able safely to negotiate more backcountry roads.

For all highway-type recreation vehicles, site selection is basically a matter of finding a level place to park well off of the highway or road right-of-way that has the desired scenic qualities. Such vehicles minimize concern over weather, terrain and other variables.

Site selection for primitive camping from other vehicles, with or without off-road capabilities, or from backpacks, requires more care because of natural hazards. During the windy months, sites that are sheltered by trees or large rock outcroppings offer some protection. Whenever rain is possible, sites near stream courses that could flash-flood should be avoided.

Sites that may be frequented by wild or domestic animals, such as springs, can be hazardous or annoying. In the warmer months, well-watered areas in the desert or mountains, or the shores of lakes, rivers or streams, may be infested with biting insects or unpleasant plants such as nettles or poison oak.

Domestic animals, such as cattle, horses or sheep, will generally avoid people in the backcountry, but areas that such animals frequent do not make pleasant or sanitary campsites. This is a major problem in canyon country, where aesthetic, recreational, watershed and other values are diminished on so-called "multiple-use" public land by the grazing of domestic livestock.

The terrain, itself, can be a hazard that should be considered during campsite selection in canyon country. Families with children should avoid proximity to cliffs or dangerous drops. Places within range of rock falls should be avoided by everyone, even those camping in recreation vehicles. Areas where there are "living" sand dunes can also be hazardous or very uncomfortable if winds come up. Backpackers, who have minimal equipment for protection from natural annoyances and hazards, should take special care in selecting campsites. For more information about noxious plants, insects, wildlife and other natural hazards in canyon country, see "Canyon Country Hiking & Natural History."

Tent campers, whatever their mode of transportation, will find problems with setting tent pegs in canyon country, except in the mountains. Much of the lower terrain is either too sandy to hold tent pegs firmly, or too rocky to permit them to be driven.

There are other general hazards to primitive camping on the land in canyon country. In the dry season, forest or brush fires could be hazardous in some areas, and camping fires should be handled with great care. Camping is inadvisable in areas being subjected to mineral search and development. The heavy machinery and explosives commonly used with these activities make the vicinity dangerous, especially since the laws regarding the uses of explosives are very loosely enforced in canyon country.

Most of the water in the canyon country hinterlands is polluted enough to be a health hazard. Some water sources, such as certain springs, may have mineral content that can cause gastro-intestinal upset. A few actually contain poisonous minerals. The greatest source of dangerous pollution, however, is from grazing domestic animals. Any source of water that such animals can reach should be considered polluted.

The rivers of canyon country are exceptionally high in both mineral and biological pollutants, as are most of the perennial flowing streams. Only a few of the more remote and vigorous mountain streams can be considered safe to drink without treatment.

It is recommended that campers carry along their own water supplies from safe sources. When this is not practical, as with backpackers or prolonged backcountry vehicle camping, all local water should be purified by boiling or chemical treatment. The most safe and effective treatment is boiling followed by chemical treatment, then filtration through activated charcoal. Several commercial firms offer kits for chemical treatment and filtration.

River runners, or boat campers on Lake Powell, who cannot take along enough water to last for their entire trip should also treat the water they take from the lake or river for cooking or drinking purposes.

Another hazard for primitive campers to avoid is the deer hunting season. During that few-day period each fall, it is safer for non-hunters to avoid all camping in the mountains or higher, wooded elevations, and to camp only in the more open desert areas away from river bottoms, canyon-streams and the denser pinyon-juniper forests in the mid-elevations. In a few areas, there are also short hunting seasons for elk, bear, bison, antelope and game birds. These areas are also best avoided by non-hunters during those seasons. Local visitor centers can usually supply current details concerning hunting areas and seasons.

Primitive camping should also be avoided on posted private land, except with the owner's prior permission. Since public land is so abundant in canyon country, there is no need to trespass on private land, for camping or any other purpose, except to cross it on established roads and trails.

Within the general Moab vicinity, the five off-road vehicle trail guidebooks listed in the back of this book note some suggested primitive campsites in their various trail descriptions.

Primitive campsite selection along canyon country rivers is more restricted than with general land camping. Highways and roads closely parallel some stretches of the rivers, allowing vehicle travelers to camp beside the water in some places. For the most part, site selection beside rivers for vehicle travelers is limited by access from the road, and level places to park. Some such sites are noted in the highway camping charts later in this guidebook.

Site selection for river runners is far less limited, but is still usually restricted by the scarcity of suitable ground that is close enough to the river. Dense willow, tamarisk and other vegetation crowd many riverbank sites that might otherwise be suitable for camping, and during the warmer months such overgrown areas harbor biting insects. Other long stretches of river are dominated by sheer cliffs or rocky talus slopes that preclude camping.

Thus, along rivers, the more open sandbars and embankments, and even rock shelves, make the best primitive campsites. During inclement weather, however, low sandbars should be avoided because of possible flooding. Other canyon country guidebooks offer more details concerning river running and access to canyon country rivers by off-road vehicles.

It is also possible to camp from vehicles along the shores of Lake Powell in some places. Again, site selection depends largely upon access to the lake from the highways and roads. Some such sites are noted in the highway camping charts later in this book.

Site selection for boat camping on Lake Powell depends to some extent upon personal tastes, although there are a few natural hazards that must be considered.

Some people prefer to camp on sandy beaches, or have never learned to do otherwise, but as the reservoir's water is drawn down each summer and fall, it carries loose sand and gravel down with it, leaving fewer sandy beaches each year as the water level rises again in the spring.

Where sandy beaches exist, they are often exposed to severe wave action when winds blow, and have submerged plants and cacti just off shore that make swimming unpleasant or hazardous. The best sandy beaches are small ones nestled in protected side canyons, or hidden within areas where slickrock domes form shoreline coves. Such sites are often free of vegetation and afford protection from winds and wave action, but may have underwater rock hazards.

Boaters who are more experienced with camping on this unique desert lake find that a gently-sloping slickrock shoreline makes a good campsite, especially if it is in a protected side canyon or cove. Although such sites require care to avoid underwater rock, and may present mooring or beaching problems for larger boats, they usually offer excellent on-shore camping, driftwood for fires, good hiking nearby, little blowing sand, and firm bottoms and clear water for swimming.

Beached boats can either be pulled up on the little patches of loose sand that are often found between slickrock domes, or pulled up onto pieces of driftwood to protect their hulls from rock abrasion. On-shore boat mooring is usually to nearby trees, boulders, ledges or large shrubs. Off-shore anchoring generally is no problem, unless the bottom is a shallow layer of sand on solid rock.

Some Lake Powell boaters prefer still another approach to campsite selection. This involves choosing one of the many interesting side canyons, then finding either a shore campsite along the canyon or at its upper end, or simply mooring to a cliff wall somewhere, or anchoring offshore, if the water is not too deep.

Side canyon camping has both advantages and hazards. It offers protection from wind and wind-generated waves, but leaves the boat and campsite exposed to the wakes of passing boats. With the larger boats that are common on Lake Powell, this can be quite troublesome, even when they pass at slow speeds. During the warmer months, side canyon camping also offers protection from the hot sun, but in many side canyons the water is more heavily clouded by algae, especially toward their upper ends, detracting somewhat from swimming. Further, most side canyons are too narrow to permit water sports such as skiing from the campsite, but are favored by fishermen who prefer the deep, relatively calm water there.

Camping in side canyons by simply anchoring, or mooring to a cliff wall, is only practical for those with eating and sleeping facilities aboard their boats. It is also subject to wave action and is more hazardous for children, making it inappropriate for many campers.

Lake Powell boat camping with larger self-contained craft, such as houseboats or cabin cruisers, is largely a matter of personal taste, except that finding a mooring or anchoring site safe from winds and wave action is essential. Large, heavy boats can be severely damaged if they are forced into rocks by the night winds and waves that are fairly common on Lake Powell. With careful steering, slow speeds and attention to water depth and underwater hazards, it is possible to beach, moor or anchor even the largest houseboats and cabin cruisers in one of the many sheltered coves on the main body of Lake Powell, and it is easy to find secure beach or anchor sites up most of the many long side canyons of this unique lake.

Site Cleanup

One thing is important to primitive camping in canyon country, whether on land, riverbank or lakeshore, whether from vehicle, rubber raft or backpack, and that is, LEAVE THE CAMPSITE AS CLEAN AND NATURAL AS POSSIBLE.

Lovely, unspoiled primitive campsites abound in canyon country, sites that are absolutely unique in their natural beauty and totally unspoiled by man. Enjoy their novelty and beauty, but LEAVE THEM UNSPOILED.

It is quite possible to pull off of a highway, road or trail into some beautiful little natural campsite, park, put up a tent, cook a meal, take care of natural human functions, use a little firewood if appropriate, spend a night or two, then LEAVE THAT SITE AS BEAUTIFUL AND NATURAL AS IT WAS -- with no litter, smoldering fire, partially burned trash, broken or chopped trees or shrubs, half-buried cans and bottles, or human waste and toilet paper left behind to spoil the area for others.

It is possible and easy to visit a lovely, natural setting in the mountains, beside a lake, river or stream, on a high plateau or canyon rim, in a gnarled and ancient pinyon-juniper forest or in a slickrock fin wilderness, spend a night there sharing its beauty, quiet and solitude with its wild inhabitants, and then leave that site completely unspoiled, with NOTHING LEFT BEHIND but foot and wheel tracks that the next wind or rain can erase.

True, those who are exploring the canyon country hinterlands for the purpose of savoring its beauty, novelty and mystery, will all too often find its beauty senselessly abused, damaged, or even totally destroyed, by "multiple-use" users who see nothing in this unique land but the chance to wrest personal gain from its fragile terrain.

Drastic erosion caused by decades of overgrazing by domestic animals has devastated many desert valleys and canyons. "Grazing enhancement" and "forest management" programs have leveled vast areas of virgin forest, destroying wildlife, watershed, aesthetic, recreational and other values in the process. Bulldozers and drill rigs in search of elusive minerals have created terrible long-lasting scars on the face of this land, often leaving hideous, abandoned structures and trash dumps behind them on public land, all under the banners of "free enterprise" and "energy shortage."

With all of this misuse, abuse, neglect and destruction by the traditional users of public land, recreational users have every right to wonder why they should be careful to preserve the beauty of the land, when its commercial users and administrators are not.

Perhaps this can be explained by saying that civilized people respect and care for the land, and will do all they can to preserve its beauty and other values, especially when that land is unique and belongs equally to everyone in this nation. It is to be hoped that those who read this book will be this civilized, and avoid adding to the damage being done by those less civilized.

Highway 191, the main route through canyon country, crosses the Colorado River at Moab.

Camping Charts By Highway

Chart Format

Type: One or more of the four general types of camping is noted for each site: OHP for off-highway overnight parking; CCG for commercial campground; PCG for public campground; PC for primitive camping
Turnoff: The number of miles from the nearest crossroad, town or other major landmark to the turnoff is given
Location: The location of the camping site is given, plus its approximate distance from the highway
Directions: Brief directions for reaching the camping site are given, beginning at the highway turnoff indicated
Comments: Any comments or personal observations of the guidebook author are listed here
Note: Chart users should note that while all commercial and public campgrounds within practical range of each highway for overnight use are listed, only representative or general off-highway parking and primitive sites are listed.

Interstate 70 & U.S. 50, Between Grand Junction and Salina, 203 Miles

TYPE	TURNOFF	LOCATION	DIRECTIONS	COMMENTS
$ CCG	Into town of Grand Junction	In Grand Junction south of freeway	Leave I-70 at any of six interchanges; watch for CCG signs or inquire locally.	Most commercial campgrounds are on the approach roads, U.S. 6 and U.S. 50, outside town.
PCG	10 Miles from Grand Junction	In Colorado National Monument, 4 miles	Leave I-70 at Fruita interchange, follow signs to monument campground.	Steep grade into monument.
OHP	47 miles from Grand Junction	Beside old highway loop to Cisco, 0 to 10 miles	Leave I-70 at interchange about 17 miles west of Colorado-Utah border.	Rejoin I-70 or go south on Utah 128, just west of Cisco.
OHP	56 miles from Grand Junction	Beside frontage road south of I-70, 0 to 2 miles	Leave I-70 at Cisco interchange, then get onto gravel frontage road on south side of freeway.	Many off-highway parking sites beside frontage road and other roads into open desert.
OHP	66 miles from Grand Junction	Beside Yellowcat Road, south from I-70, 0 to 7 miles	Leave I-70 at ranch interchange, then take gravel road south.	Off-highway parking beside gravel road south.
OHP	72 miles from Grand Junction	Beside Thompson Road south from I-70, 0 to 7 miles	Leave I-70 at Thompson interchange, then take gravel road south.	Off-highway parking beside gravel road south. Rejoin I-70 or continue south to U.S. 191.
PC	6 miles west of Crescent Junction	Beside Floy Wash Road south from I-70, 0 to 15 miles	Leave I-70 at Floy Wash Road, then take dirt road south.	Off-highway parking beside dirt road south, good primitive desert camping beyond 4 miles.

PC OHP	15 miles west of Crescent Junction	Beside Crystal Geyser Road south from I-70, 0 to 5 miles	Leave I-70 at Crystal Geyser Road, then take road south.	Off-highway parking beside road south, primitive camping beside Green River beyond 5 miles.
$ CCG PCG	In town of Green River	PCG in Green River State Park, 1/2 mile south of I-70, CCG in town	Leave I-70 at sign between river and town, follow signs to campground.	Watch for commercial campground signs or inquire locally for directions.
OHP	At I-70, Utah 24 interchange	Just north of interchange, at base of bluff	Leave I-70 at Utah 24 interchange, park in area north of interchange.	Other off-highway parking farther north and beside Utah 24 to the south.
PC PCG OHP	18 miles west of I-70/U24 interchange	BLM campground 7 miles north of I-70; off-highway parking, 0 to 5 miles north or south; primitive camping north or south	Leave I-70 at ranch interchange, head north to public campground, north or south for off-highway parking or primitive camping.	Unpaved roads north and south from interchange enter highly scenic San Rafael Swell area.
OHP	35 miles west of I-70/U24 interchange	Beside road northwest, 0 to 7 miles	Leave I-70 at Moore interchange, take road northwest toward Moore.	Return to I-70 or continue to Moore and Utah 10.
OHP	At I-70, Utah 10 interchange	Beside roads north or south, 0 to 5 miles	Leave I-70 at U10 interchange, head north on U10 or south on dirt road.	

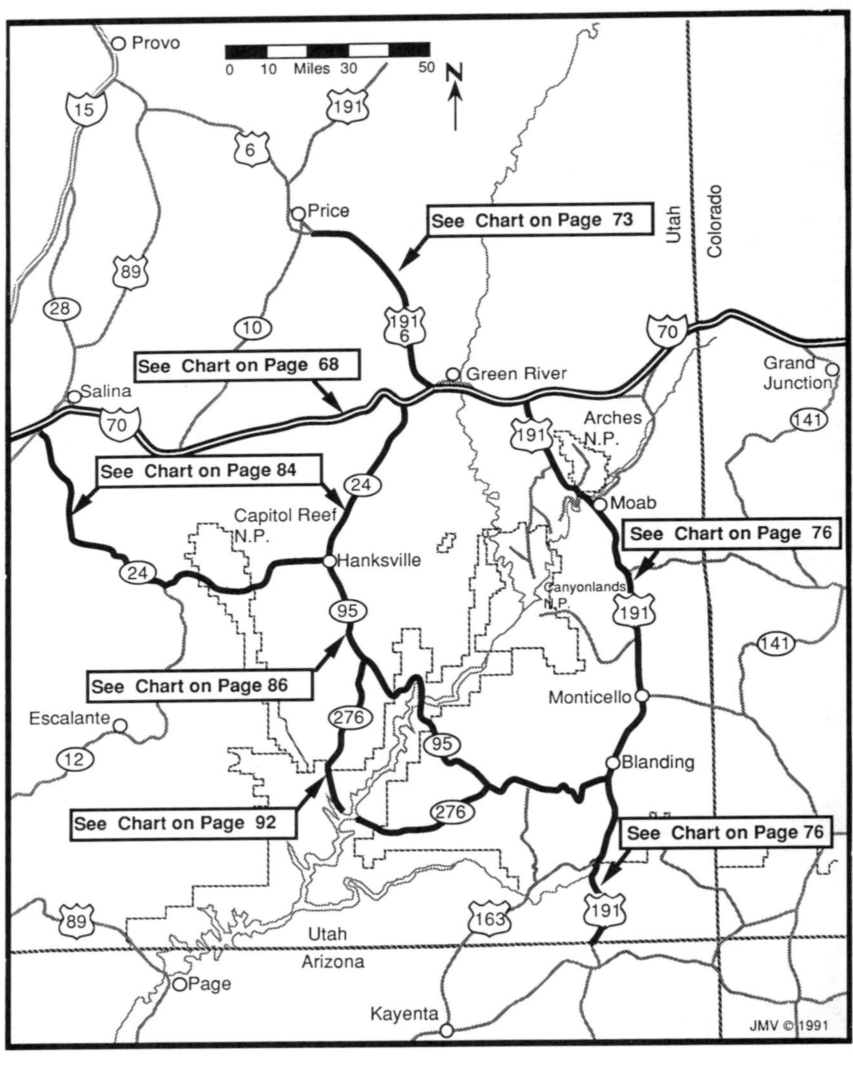

Highway Locator Map - Main Through Routes

View from turnout along Interstate 70

Interstate 70 continued

PC OHP	At I-70, Utah 72 interchange	Beside U72 south, 0 to 20 miles	Leave I-70 at U72 interchange, head south on U72.	Off-highway parking first several miles, primitive camping in National Forest. Grades.
PC OHP	16 miles west of I-70/U72 interchange	Beside roads north, 0 to 20 miles	Leave I-70 at interchange, head north on dirt road.	Off-highway parking, primitive camping in National Forest. PCG's farther north. Grades.
PC PCG OHP	27 miles west of I-70/U72 interchange	U.S.F.S. campground 10 miles south of I-70. Off-highway parking & primitive camping 0 to 10 miles	Leave I-70 at interchange, head south on paved and dirt road, follow signs to public campground.	
$ CCG	In town of Salina	In Salina, 2 miles beyond end of I-70 & U.S. 50 freeway	Watch for CCG signs on I-70/U.S. 50 or inquire locally for directions.	Commercial campgrounds in Salina are small.

U.S. 6, Between Price and the U.S. 6/Interstate 70 Junction, 57 Miles

TYPE	TURNOFF	LOCATION	DIRECTIONS	COMMENTS
$ CCG	In town	In Price, near highway	Watch for CCG signs on U.S. 6 or inquire locally for directions.	
PC OHP	2 miles east of Wellington	OHP beside road north, 0 to 4 miles; primitive camping near the road, beyond 4 miles	Turn north on paved then dirt road.	Off-highway parking first 4 miles, primitive camping beyond in higher elevations. Avoid private ranch lands.
OHP	0 to 57 miles from Price	Near road many places between Price and I-70	Watch for leveled areas well off of highway, or beside spur dirt roads.	Numerous off-highway parking sites in this stretch of desert.

U.S. 89, Between Kanab and the U.S. 89/U.S. 160 Junction, 152 Miles

TYPE	TURNOFF	LOCATION	DIRECTIONS	COMMENTS
$ CCG	In town	In Kanab, near highway	Watch for CCG signs on highway, or inquire locally for directions.	
$ CCG	Near town	North of town in Glen County	Watch for CCG about 6 miles north of town	
PCG	Near Arizona-Utah border	Lone Rock, on Wahweap Bay, Lake Powell, about 2 miles from highway	Turn east on dirt road about 7 miles south of town of Glen Canyon.	Campground near lake, but undeveloped except for toilets.
$ CCG PCG	13 miles south of town of Glen Canyon	Wahweap Campground, on Wahweap Bay, Lake Powell; CCG nearby	Turn east on paved road about 13 miles south of Glen Canyon, or 6 miles north of Page, follow signs to PCG or CCG.	Campgrounds can also be approached via lakeshore drive from Glen Canyon Dam visitor center.
$ CCG	In town	In Page, near highway	Watch for CCG signs on highway, or inquire locally for directions.	
PC OHP	0 to 152 miles from Kanab	OHP near road many places between Kanab and U.S. 89/U.S. 160 junction; PC in nearby desert backcountry within Utah	For OHP, watch for leveled areas well off of highway or beside spur dirt roads; for PC take any of numerous spur dirt roads from highway into Utah backcountry.	Numerous off-highway parking sites between Kanab and Page; Navajo Indian reservation south of Page in Arizona, OHP, PC not recommended.

Roadside Camping Along Highway 191

U.S. 191, Between Crescent Junction and Kayenta, 204 Miles

TYPE	TURNOFF	LOCATION	DIRECTIONS	COMMENTS
PCG	21 miles south of Crescent Junction	Dead Horse Point State Park, 22 miles from highway	Drive west on Utah 313; campground is within park, near visitor center.	Short steep grade about 3 miles from U.S. 191.
PCG	27 miles south of Crescent Junction	Devils Garden campground, Arches National Park, 17 miles from U.S. 191	Drive into park to Devils Garden area at end of paved road; campground loop road starts here.	Check at park entrance station or visitor center for site availability before driving to campground. Steep grade first mile.
$ CCG	Near or within town	Along Highway 191 in or near Moab,	Watch for CCG signs on highway, or inquire locally for directions.	CCGs within Moab on or near highway; beside highway, north and south of town.
PCG	12 miles south of La Sal Junction	Wind Whistle Campground; about 6 miles from U.S. 191	Drive west on paved road that leaves U.S. 191 about 12 miles south of La Sal Junction; campground is beside road.	Watch for Canyon Rims Recreation Area sign on highway.
PCG	18 miles south of La Sal Junction	Newspaper Rock State Historical Monument; about 12 miles from U.S. 191	Drive west on paved Utah 211; campground is at monument beside road.	Limited campsites. Steep down-grade just east of monument.
$ CCG PCG	In town, and 5 and 6 miles west	CCG in Monticello near highway; PCG in nearby national forest, Dalton Springs, 5 miles, Buckboard 6 miles	Watch for CCG signs on highway, or inquire locally for directions; drive west on paved road, follow signs to national forest campgrounds.	Grades in national forest.

PCG	11 miles south of Monticello	Devils Canyon campground, 1/2 mile from highway	Watch for U.S. Forest Service campground sign on highway.	
$ CCG	In and south of town	In Blanding and south of town	Watch for CCG signs on highway or inquire locally for directions.	
$ CCG	In town	In Bluff, near highway	Watch for CCG signs on highway or inquire locally for directions.	
PCG	3-1/2 miles west of Bluff	Sand Island campground about 1/2 mile from U.S. 191	Drive south on dirt road from sign on highway to campground.	Limited development.
PCG	22 miles west of Bluff	Goosenecks of the San Juan State Reserve; about 4-1/2 miles from U.S. 163	Drive north on Utah 261 for about one mile, then west at sign to Goosenecks campground.	Campground largely undeveloped; no water.
$ CCG	In town	In Mexican Hat, near highway	Watch for CCG signs on highway, or inquire locally for directions.	
$ CCG	21 miles south-west of Mexican Hat	In Monument Valley, at Gouldings Trading Post, 2 miles from U.S. 191	Turn toward Gouldings Trading Post at sign on U.S. 191 follow signs to campground.	
$ CCG	Near town	Near Kayenta, at U.S. 191/U.S. 160 junction	Watch for CCG signs on highway, or inquire locally for directions.	

OHP	15 to 150 miles, from Crescent Junction to San Juan River	OHP near road many places between Canyonlands Air Field and San Juan River	Watch for leveled areas well off of highway, or beside spur dirt roads.	Numerous off-highway parking sites between Canyonlands Air Field and the San Juan River; Navajo Indian reservation south of San Juan River, OHP not recommended.
PC	0 to 150 miles from Crescent Junction to San Juan River	Primitive camping in nearby desert-canyon backcountry north of San Juan River, near highway	Take any of numerous spur dirt roads from highway into backcountry.	Navajo Indian reservation south of San Juan River, primitive camping not recommended.

U.S. 160, Between Cortez and the U.S. 160/U.S. 89 Junction, 200 Miles

TYPE	TURNOFF	LOCATION	DIRECTIONS	COMMENTS
$ CCG	In town	In Cortez, near highway	Watch for CCG signs on highway, or inquire locally for directions.	
$ CCG	Near town	Near U.S. 160/U.S. 191 junction, near the town of Kayenta	Watch for CCG signs on highway or inquire locally for directions.	
PCG	9 miles south-west of Tsegi	Navajo National Monument, 9 miles north of highway	Watch for monument sign on highway; follow signs to monument campground.	

OHP	0 to 200 miles	OHP near road many places between Cortez and U.S. 160/U.S. 89 junction	Watch for leveled areas well off of highway, or beside spur dirt roads.	Many off-highway parking sites in this remote stretch of desert, some provided by Arizona highway department.

U.S. 666, Between Cortez and Monticello, 60 Miles

TYPE	TURNOFF	LOCATION	DIRECTIONS	COMMENTS
$ CCG	In town	In Cortez, near highway	Watch for CCG signs on highway, or inquire locally for directions.	
OHP	20 to 45 miles from Cortez	OHP adjacent to road can be found several places west of Pleasant View	Watch for established OHP sites beside the highway west of Pleasant View and in pinyon-juniper woods near Colorado-Utah border.	OHP not readily available in farm region between Cortez and Dove Creek in Colorado, and for the last 10 miles east of Monticello.
$ CCG PCG	In town, and 5 and 6 miles west	CCG in Monticello near highway; PCG in nearby national forest, Dalton Springs, 5 miles, Buckboard, 6 miles	Watch for CCG signs on highway, or inquire locally for directions; drive west on paved road, follow signs to national forest campgrounds.	Grades in national forest

Interstate 70 as it crosses the San Rafael Reef

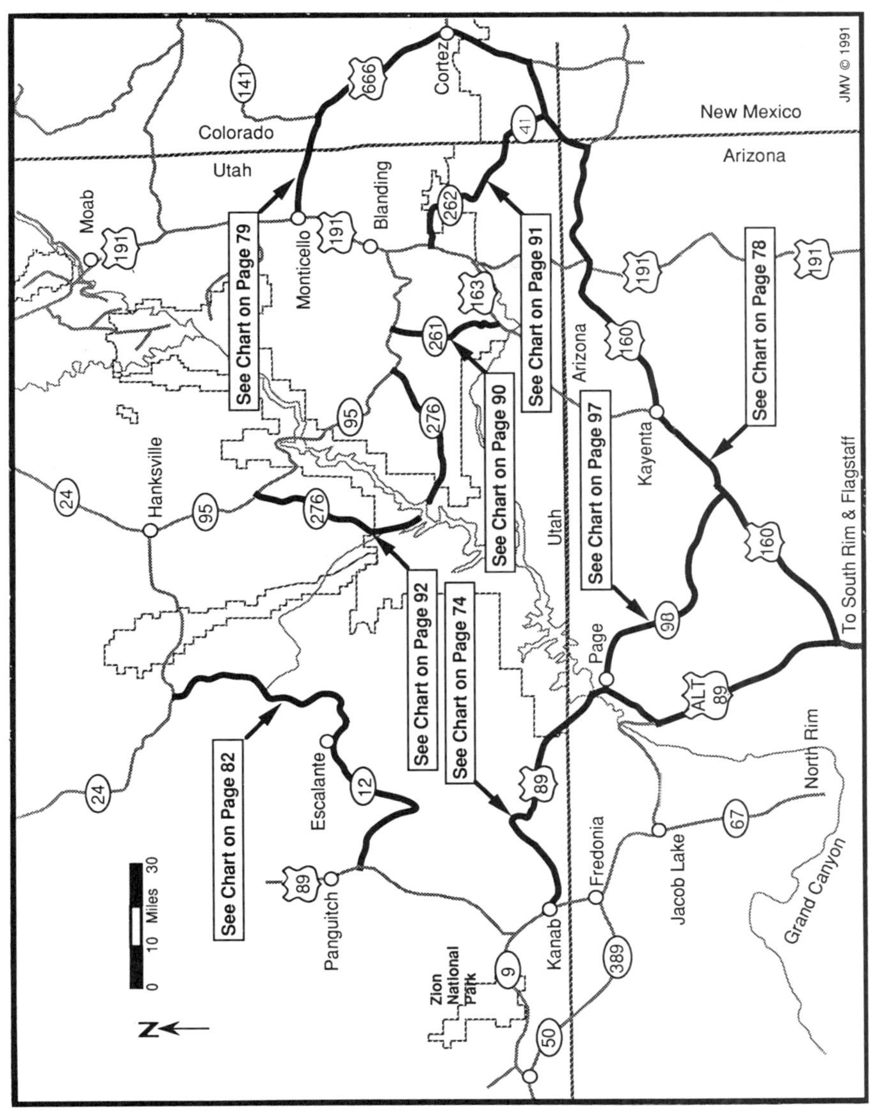

Highway Locator Map - South and West of Canyon Country

Utah 12, between Utah 12/U.S. 89 Junction and Boulder, 87 Miles

TYPE	TURNOFF	LOCATION	DIRECTIONS	COMMENTS
PCG	14 miles east of U12/U.S. 89 junction	Bryce Canyon National Park campgrounds, 3 miles from Utah 12	Turn south from U12 into park, follow signs to campgrounds.	Campgrounds may be full during summer travel season.
PCG	27 miles east of U12/U.S. 89 junction	Kodachrome Basin State Park campground, 7 miles from Utah 12	Turn south from U12 at Cannonville, on paved, then dirt, road; follow signs to state park.	20 unit developed campground, very scenic setting, water.
PCG	1 mile west of Escalante	Escalante Petrified Forest State Park, short drive north of U12	Turn north from U12 about 1 mile west of Escalante then drive improved road into state park.	Spacious camp sites near small reservoir; limited shade; hikes into petrified forest areas.
$ CCG	In Escalante	In Escalante near highway	Watch for CCG signs on highway, or inquire locally for directions.	Campground is associated with motel.
PCG	13 miles east of Escalante	Calf Creek Recreation Area campground, just off of U12	Watch for sign at turnoff into campground beside Calf Creek, about midway between Escalante and Boulder.	Small campground in very picturesque setting. Not for larger recreation vehicles.
PCG	In Boulder	In national forest, 9, 10 and 15 miles north of Boulder	Turn north in Boulder on dirt road, follow signs to Oak Creek, Pleasant Creek and Single Tree campgrounds.	Mountain grades; campgrounds all above 8600 feet elevation; not for larger recreation vehicles.

PC OHP	30 to 87 miles from U12/U.S. 89 junction	OHP adjacent to road can be found many places between Henrieville and Boulder; primitive camping in nearby backcountry	Watch for leveled areas well off of highway, or beside spur dirt roads; for primitive camping, drive on any spur road into backcountry.	Many off-highway parking sites in this remote desert canyon area, some beside streams; primitive camping excellent. Avoid private ranch lands.
PC OHP	Boulder	Beside or near dirt road east from Boulder	Watch for leveled areas well off of highway, or beside spur dirt roads; for primitive camping, follow spur roads into backcountry.	Main dirt road east, then south to Bullfrog, rough in places but safe for highway vehicles when dry. Not advisable for large recreation vehicles. Excellent primitive camping, many places.

Utah 24, Between U24/U.S. 89 Junction and the U24/I-70 Junction, 168 Miles

TYPE	TURNOFF	LOCATION	DIRECTIONS	COMMENTS
OHP	0 to 70 miles from U.S. 89	Very few OHP locations between U.S. 89 and Capitol Reef National Park	Watch for leveled areas well off of highway, or beside spur dirt roads	OHP not readily available in farm regions between U.S. 89 and Capitol Reef National Park; OHP not permitted within park.
PCG	29 miles from U.S. 89	Fish Lake, in national forest, 7 miles from U24	Leave U24 on paved U5 to Fish lake, follow signs to Bowery and Mackinaw campgrounds.	Grades. Sites may be full at these popular camp - grounds during the summer travel season.
PCG	51 miles from U.S. 89	In national forest 1 mile southeast of Bicknell near highway	Watch on highway for sign to Sunglow campground.	Very small campgrounds, no water, not for larger recreation vehicles.
PCG	70 miles from U.S. 89	In Capitol Reef National Park, 1-1/2 miles from U24	Turn south at sign by visitor center in park; follow signs on paved road to campground.	Very picturesque setting, but may be full during summer travel season.
$ CCG	In or near town	In Hanksville, beside highway	Watch for CCG signs on highway.	One CCG north of town on U24, past U24/U95 junction.

PCG	20 miles north of Hanksville	In Goblin Valley State Park, 12 miles from U24	Turn east from U24 on paved road; after 5-1/2 miles, turn south at park sign on dirt road; campground 6-1/2 miles from pavement.	6-1/2 miles of dirt road rough and sandy, but passable to highway vehicles when dry; not recommended for large recreation vehicles.
OHP	From 10 miles east of Capitol Reef N.P. to U24/I-70 junction	OHP adjacent to road can be found many places between Capitol Reef N.P. eastern boundary and I-70; PC in adjacent desert	Watch for leveled areas well off of highway, or beside spur dirt roads; for primitive camping, follow spur roads into backcountry.	Standard highway vehicles should exercise great care in leaving paved roads in this desert area, because of soft soils and sand; even on the graded roads.

Utah 95, Between the U95/U.S. 191 Junction and Hanksville, 128 miles

TYPE	TURNOFF	LOCATION	DIRECTIONS	COMMENTS
PCG	About 2 miles west of U95/U261 junction	In Natural Bridges National Monument, about 5 miles from U95 by paved road	Turn north on paved road at monument sign; paved road ends in monument; campground near visitor center.	Small campground in pinyon-juniper woods; not recommended for large recreation vehicles.
OHP	0 to 128 miles from U.S. 191	OHP adjacent to highway can be found many places along U95 for its entire length	Watch for leveled areas well off of highway, or beside spur dirt or paved roads.	Numerous scenic OHP sites beside this Bicentennial Highway.
PC	0 to 128 miles from U.S. 191	Primitive camping in the adjacent desert, canyon and forest areas	Turn off of U95 at any of many paved or dirt side roads, continue into wild backcountry.	Some dirt side roads are not suitable for standard highway vehicles, especially large recreation vehicles.
PCG	Just south of bridge over Lake Powell	Near Hite developed area and marina, beside Lake Powell	Turn off of U95 onto paved access road to Hite development; follow signs to campground.	Designated camping area, with no developed facilities.

PC OHP	1 mile south and 1/2 mile north of White Canyon Bridge; 1/2 to 1-1/2 miles west of Dirty Devil bridge	Beside or near Lake Powell at three locations, one a few yards from U95, the other two about 2 miles by dirt road	Turn west on either of two dirt roads; 1 mile south of White Canyon bridge or 1/2 mile north of bridge; stay on dirt roads for about 2 miles to White Canyon or Farleys Canyon; turn off of U95 along west side of Dirty Devil arm of Lake Powell, onto short dirt spur roads.	Two spur roads near White Canyon bridge go to OHP and PC near lake in two bays. Very scenic OHP and PC along west side of Dirty Devil arm and confluence.
$ CCG	In or near town	In Hanksville, beside highway	Watch for CCG signs on the highway.	One CCG north of town on U24 past U24/U95 junction.

Utah 128, between the U128/I-70 Junction and U128/U.S. 191 Junction, 45 Miles

TYPE	TURNOFF	LOCATION	DIRECTIONS	COMMENTS
OHP	At U128/I-70 junction	Beside frontage road south of I-70	At U128/I-70 junction, get onto frontage road heading west on south side of I-70; OHP beside gravel frontage road.	OHP beside frontage road and other dirt roads that branch south into the desert.
OHP	0 to 45 miles from I-70	Beside highway at many locations along the entire length of U128	Watch for leveled areas well off of highway, or beside spur dirt roads.	Best areas for OHP begin about 4 miles north of Dewey Bridge, across Colorado River.
PC	12 to 45 miles from I-70	PC in adjacent redrock canyon country near U128	Turn off of U128 at spur dirt roads west of Dewey Bridge, drive to scenic primitive camping locations.	Good site for primitive camping west of Dewey Bridge; up dirt road to Fisher Valley; toward river in same vicinity; at Big Bend beside river; other sites beside river in downstream narrows.
OHP	At U128/U.S. 191 junction	Beside road, adjacent to Lions Park	Park in leveled area between highway and park, at junction.	OHP not permitted in Lions Park but permitted beside highway at junction.

Utah 211, between the U211/U.S. 191 Junction and Canyonlands N.P., 33 Miles

TYPE	TURNOFF	LOCATION	DIRECTIONS	COMMENTS
OHP	3 to 33 miles from U.S. 191	OHP adjacent to highway can be found several places beginning about 3 miles from U.S. 191	Watch for leveled areas well off of highway, or beside spur dirt roads.	Do not trespass on posted private ranch lands in Indian Creek Canyon.
PCG	About 12 miles from U.S. 191	Beside highway at Newspaper Rock State Historical Monument	Watch for monument sign; campground is across road from Newspaper Rock.	Wooded, stream side setting, but small and often full during summer travel season.
PC	3 to 33 miles from U.S. 191	In nearby desert or canyon country near the highway	Take any spur dirt road into nearby backcountry if not fenced and posted.	Many dirt roads into back-country good for primitive camping, especially between Indian Creek Canyon and park boundary.
$ CCG	1 mile west of park boundary	Just outside of park, north of highway	Watch for sign just west of park boundary; take paved road north that goes to private resort outside of park.	Commercial resort and camp-ground may not always be open, especially during off-season.
PCG	3 miles beyond highway end	Squaw Flat campground in Canyonlands N.P., Needles District	Continue west on paved road into park; follow signs to campground, about 3 miles beyond park boundary.	During summer travel season, inquire at park entrance station about sites, before driving on to campground.

Utah 261, between the U261/U.S. 191 Junction and the U261/U95 Junction, 33 Miles

TYPE	TURNOFF	LOCATION	DIRECTIONS	COMMENTS
PCG	About 1 mile north of U.S. 191	Goosenecks of the San Juan State Reserve, 3-1/2 miles from U261	Watch for paved road to the west about 1 mile north of U.S. 191; campground at end of road.	Small campground, limited development, but beside rim with breathtaking overlook.
OHP	0 to 33 miles from U.S. 191	OHP adjacent to highway can be found many places along entire length of U261	Watch for leveled areas well off of highway, or beside spur dirt roads.	Best OHP north of grade up onto Cedar Mesa, in wooded areas.
PC	0 to 33 miles from U.S. 191	In nearby desert, redrock country or on wooded Cedar Mesa	Take any spur dirt road into the backcountry near the highway.	Good primitive camping in Valley of the Gods, at Muley Point and vicinity and on Cedar Mesa near rim of Johns Canyon.

Utah 262/Colorado 41, between the C41/U.S. 160 Junction and the U262/U.S. 191 Junction, 50 Miles

TYPE	TURNOFF	LOCATION	DIRECTIONS	COMMENTS
OHP	None	None	None	OHP not recommended beside or near U262 because most of it is within the Navajo Indian reservation, and in some areas oil drilling and pumping activities create hazards.
PCG	At junction 8-1/2 miles east of U.S. 191	In Hovenweep National Monument, 16 miles by paved and dirt road from U262	Follow Hovenweep signs to monument and campground.	Dirt road passable to standard highway vehicles and large recreation vehicles except when wet.

Utah 276, Between the U276/U95 Junction and Bullfrog, Lake Powell, 45 Miles

TYPE	TURNOFF	LOCATION	DIRECTIONS	COMMENTS
PCG	About 17 miles from U95	Starr Springs campground in Henry Mountains, about 3-1/2 miles from U276, by dirt road	Watch for Starr Springs sign by highway, about 17 miles from U95; follow signs to campground.	Grades, not recommended for larger recreation vehicles, or for standard highway vehicles when wet.
OHP	0 to 45 miles from U95	OHP adjacent to highway can be found a few places along U276	Watch for leveled areas well off of highway, or beside spur dirt roads.	Nearby terrain so steep or mountainous that there are few OHP sites.
PC	0 to 45 miles from U95	In nearby redrock desert	Take one of the few spur dirt roads into the nearby redrock desert.	Plenty of primitive camping near spur dirt road from U276 to Burr trail junction near Bullfrog.
$ CCG PCG	At end of highway	Bullfrog campground, near Bullfrog developed area and marina, beside Lake Powell; CCG nearby	Near end of paved highway within recreation area, follow signs to public campground; CCG nearby.	

Utah 276, between the U276/U95 Junction and Halls Crossing, Lake Powell, 44 Miles

TYPE	TURNOFF	LOCATION	DIRECTIONS	COMMENTS
OHP	0 to 44 miles from U95	OHP adjacent to highway can be found many places along entire length of U276	Watch for leveled areas well off of highway, or beside spur dirt roads.	Best OHP is in higher pass about 22 miles from U95.
PC	0 to 44 miles from U95	In nearby desert or slickrock country	Take any dirt spur road into the desert backcountry near the highway.	Best primitive camping is in the vicinity of the higher pass about 22 miles from U95.
$ CCG PCG	At end of highway	Near Halls Crossing developed area and marina beside Lake Powell; CCG nearby	Near end of paved highway within recreation area; follow signs to public campground; CCG nearby.	

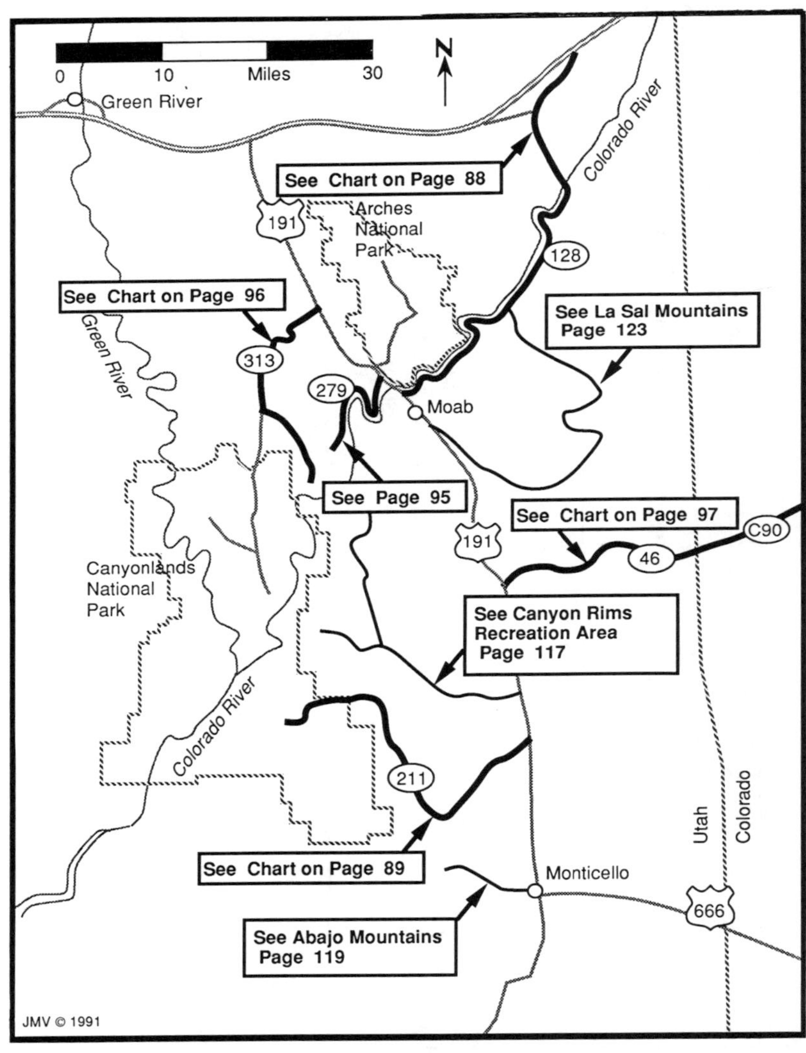

Highway Locator Map - Moab Area Detail

Utah 279, Between the U279/U.S. 191 Junction and Potash, 15 Miles

TYPE	TURNOFF	LOCATION	DIRECTIONS	COMMENTS
PC OHP	3 to 14 miles from U.S. 191	OHP and primitive camping beside highway, within river gorge	There are several sites for OHP or primitive camping beside the highway between The Portal and the Potash Mill at the end of U279 pavement; still more near dirt road that continues beyond pavement.	Best sites between highway and cliffs, between 3 and 5 miles from U.S. 191 also good up Long Canyon Trail just south of Jughandle Arch.
PCG	13 miles from U.S. 191	At Dead Horse Point State Park, about 12 miles by dirt road and off-road vehicle trail	Turn into Long Canyon just south of Jughandle Arch; at end of dirt road and ORV trail, go sharp left on paved Utah 313 to park; follow signs to campground.	Standard highway vehicles can travel dirt road for about 3 miles; off-road vehicles only can reach summit of Long Canyon road/trail and Dead Horse Point by this route, without trailers.

Utah 313, Between the U313/U.S. 191 Junction and Dead Horse Point, 22 Miles

TYPE	TURNOFF	LOCATION	DIRECTIONS	COMMENTS
PC OHP	0 to 16 miles from U.S. 191	Many sites for OHP or primitive camping beside or near the highway, to the state park boundary	Watch for leveled areas well off of highway, or beside spur dirt roads; primitive camping in backcountry entered by all spur roads and trails.	Best OHP, PC in canyon, first 3 miles; not permitted within state park; short, steep grade about 3 miles from U.S. 191 passable by all vehicles, with care.
PCG	Near end of highway	In Dead Horse Point State Park, in developed area near visitor center	Follow signs from paved road to campground.	Excellent campground, but may be full during summer travel season.

Utah 46/Colorado 90 between the C90/C141 Junction and La Sal Junction, 55 Miles

TYPE	TURNOFF	LOCATION	DIRECTIONS	COMMENTS
OHP	0 to 55 miles from C90/C141 junction	OHP adjacent to road can be found several places along U24/C90	Watch for leveled areas well off of highway, or beside spur dirt roads.	Some OHP in high wooded setting east of town of La Sal.
PC	First 10 miles west of Colorado/Utah border	National forest to the north of U46, various distances from highway	Watch for graded dirt roads to the north within the eastern 10 miles of Utah; drive into wooded region.	Do not enter posted private ranch lands in this stretch; public roads are open, with no fences or gates.

Arizona 98, Between the A98/U.S. 160 Junction and Page, 66 Miles

TYPE	TURNOFF	LOCATION	DIRECTIONS	COMMENTS
PC OHP	None	None	None	OHP and PC not recommended beside or near A98 because it is entirely within the Navajo Indian Reservation.
$ CCG	In town	In Page, at end of highway	Watch for CCG signs on highway, or inquire locally for directions.	For other CCG or public grounds near Page, see U.S. 89 chart.

Owachomo Natural Bridge, Natural Bridges National Monument

Camping Charts By Special Area

Chart Format

Chart Heading: Each chart is headed by the name of the special area it summarizes
Type: Each of the four general types of camping is listed for each special area: OHP for off-highway overnight parking; CCG for commercial campgrounds; PCG for public campgrounds; and PC for primitive camping, whether from land vehicle, boat or backpack; all established sites within each special area for each type of camping are listed.
Name: The name of the camping site is given, if any; for public campgrounds, the same names listed in the campground descriptions earlier in this book are used in these charts.
Location: The general location of each site is given, within the special area being summarized; the campground descriptions earlier in this book are referenced for location details and directions, whenever appropriate.
Accessibility: Accessibility by various types of vehicles is given for each site, as recommended by the author of this guidebook.
Route: The general route to each site is given, using established highway numbers, and the names of backcountry roads and trails standardized in various Canyon Country offroad vehicle trail guidebooks and maps; the exact locations of some backcountry campsites are given in these guidebooks.
Comments: Miscellaneous comments or observations by the author are listed here.

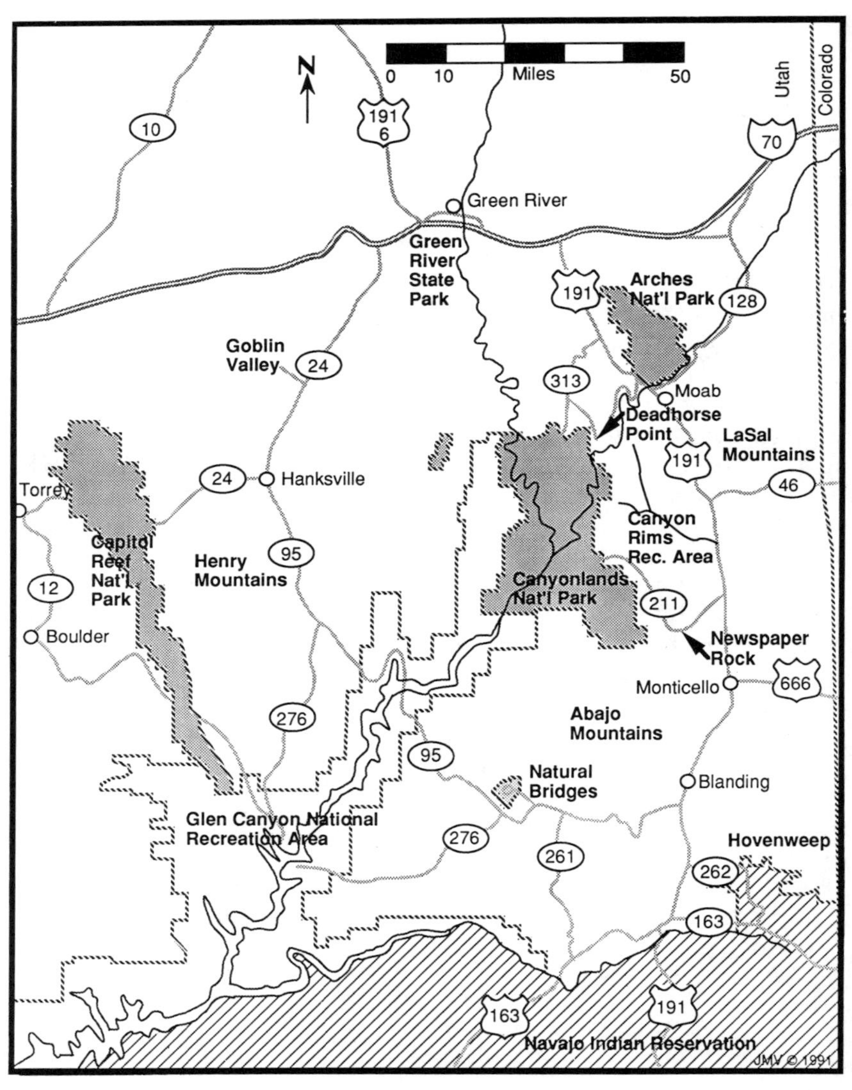

Special Areas Map

Arches National Park

TYPE	NAME	LOCATION	ACCESS	ROUTE	COMMENTS
OHP					Off-highway overnight parking is not permitted within the national park.
$ CCG					There are no commercial campgrounds within this park. The nearest are in Moab, beginning 3 miles from the park entrance.
PCG	Devils Garden	End of paved park road; see campground description	All vehicles	U.S. 191, Arches Road	Inquire at park entrance concerning site availability.
PC					Primitive camping from vehicles is not permitted within the park, but is permitted by backpackers except near developed areas.

Canyonlands National Park

TYPE	NAME	LOCATION	ACCESS	ROUTE	COMMENTS
OHP					Off-highway overnight parking is not permitted within the national park.
$ CCG					There are no commercial camp-grounds within this park. The nearest are at a resort near the Needles District entrance, or in Moab, Monticello and Hanksville for various districts.
PCG	Squaw Flat	Needles District; see campground description	All vehicles	U 211	Inquire at park entrance concerning site availability.
PCG	Willow Flat	Island in the Sky District; see campground description	All except large recreation vehicles	U 313, Island Road	Small campground, limited development, no water.
PC	Angel Arch, Peek-a-Boo	Needles District	Off-road vehicles only	U 211, Salt Creek Canyon Trail	Designated primitive sites for use by off-road vehicles; limited facilities; possible water at Peek-a-Boo only.

PCG	Goose-berry Canyon, Hardscrabble Bottom, Lathrop Canyon, Murphy Hogback, Potato Bottom	Island in the Sky District, along White Rim Trail	Off-road vehicles only	U 313, White Rim Trail	Designated primitive sites for use by off-road vehicles; no water; limited facilities at Lathrop Canyon only; see various maps for exact locations.
PC	Devils Kitchen	Needles District	Off-road vehicles only	U211, Elephant Hill Trail	Designated primitive site for use by off-road vehicles; limited facilities; no water.
PCG	Split Top Cave	Needles District	All except large recreation vehicles	U 211, Salt Creek Canyon trail	Designated group site with limited facilities; water at Squaw Flat campground, 1 mile.
PCG	Squaw Slot	Needles District	All except large recreation vehicles	U 211	Designated group site with limited facilities; water at Squaw Flat campground, 1/2 mile.
PC	Horseshoe Canyon	Maze District, Horseshoe Canyon park annex	Off-road vehicles only	U 24, Maze Road	Designated primitive site for use by off-road vehicles; creek or spring water requires purification.

PC	Indian Cave, Lizard Rock, Maze Overlook, Mother and Child	Maze District	Off-road vehicles only	U 24, Maze Road	Designated primitive sites for use by off-road vehicles; no facilities or water.
PC	Colorado River, Green River	Riverbanks	Watercraft	Rivers	Primitive campsites may be designated within the park; no facilities or water; if not designated, use any suitable site.
PC		Entire Park	Backpackers	Hiking trails or routes	Backpackers are permitted to primitive camp anywhere within the park except near developed areas, including at primitive sites designated for vehicles.

Needles District, Canyonlands National Park

Capitol Reef National Park

TYPE	NAME	LOCATION	ACCESS	ROUTE	COMMENTS
OHP					Off highway overnight parking is not permitted within the park.
$ CCG					There are no commercial campgrounds within this park. The nearest are at Hanksville, 35 miles east of the park
PCG	Capitol Reef	Near visitor center; see campground description	All vehicles	U 24, park road	Inquire at visitor center concerning site availability.
PC		Beside Notom-Bullfrog Road, north of Burr Trail turnoff	All except large recreation vehicles	U 24 or U 276, Notom-Bullfrog Road	Designated primitive site for all vehicles; limited facilities, no water; access roads may be rough and eroded in places.
PC		South Desert, Water-pocket Fold	Off-road vehicles only	South Desert trail or Burr Trail	Primitive camping from off-road vehicles is permitted north of Cathedral Valley and in Upper Muley Twist Canyon at the hiking trail head.
PC		Entire park	Backpackers	Hiking trails or routes	Backpackers are permitted to primitive camp anywhere within the park except near developed areas, including at primitive sites designated for vehicles.

Hovenweep National Monument

TYPE	NAME	LOCATION	ACCESS	ROUTE	COMMENTS
OHP					Off-highway overnight parking is not permitted within the monument.
$ CCG					There are no commercial camp-grounds within the monument. The nearest are at Blanding, 40 miles northwest of the monument.
PCG	Hoven-weep	Near Square Tower Ruin; see campground description	All vehicles	U 262, Hatch Road	Dirt access road may not be accessible to standard highway vehicles when wet.
PC					The several units of this monument are each too small to permit primitive camping from vehicles. Primitive camping may be permitted along hiking trails in non-developed units; check with monument rangers for current regulations.

Natural Bridges National Monument

TYPE	NAME	LOCATION	ACCESS	ROUTE	COMMENTS
OHP					Off-highway overnight parking is not permitted within the monument.
$ CCG					There are no commercial camp-grounds within the monument.
PCG	Natural Bridges	Near monument visitor center; see camp-ground description	All except large recreation vehicles	U 95, paved spur into monument	Inquire at visitor center concerning site availability.
PC					Primitive camping from vehicles is not permitted within the monument, but is permitted by back-packers within the two major canyons.

Rainbow Bridge National Monument

TYPE	NAME	LOCATION	ACCESS	ROUTE	COMMENTS
OHP					There is no land vehicle access into the monument.
PCG $ CCG					There are no commercial or public campgrounds within the monument. The nearest are at Wahweap, Bullfrog and Halls Crossing, each about 50 miles away by boat on Lake Powell.
PC					No primitive camping of any sort is permitted within the monument, but is permissible on the nearby lake.

Glen Canyon National Recreation Area - Lake Powell

TYPE	NAME	LOCATION	ACCESS	ROUTE	COMMENTS
OHP			All vehicles	U.S. 89, U 95, U 263, U 276	Off-highway overnight parking is permitted beside all highways that enter the recreation area, but may be impractical along some stretches. See individual highway camping charts.
$ CCG		Wahweap, Halls Crossing, Bullfrog Marina	All vehicles	U.S. 89, U 263, U 276 and park access roads	There are commercial campgrounds near each of the noted marinas and at Page and Hanksville in the general Lake Powell Vicinity
PCG	Bullfrog, Halls Crossing, Hite, Wahweap, Lees Ferry	Bullfrog, Halls Crossing, Hite and Wahweap marinas; and below the dam; see camp-ground description	All vehicles, plus boats at Hite and Lees Ferry	U.S. 89, U.S. 89A, U 263, U 276 and park access roads	Campgrounds at Hite and Lees Ferry are near enough to the water for use by boaters. Others are 1/2 mile to 1 mile from the lake
PC	Lone Rock	Wahweap Bay	All vehicles and boats	U.S. 89 and park road	Designated primitive site for all vehicles and boats; limited facilities; no water
PC		Entire lakeshore	All boats	Lake	Primitive shoreline camping is permitted anywhere on Lake Powell except in developed areas

PC		Backcountry	Off-road vehicles and backpackers	Off-road vehicle trails and hiking routes	Primitive camping is permitted beside designated trails from off-road vehicles, and anywhere by backpackers, within the backcountry of Glen Canyon National Recreation Area

Dead Horse Point State Park

TYPE	NAME	LOCATION	ACCESS	ROUTE	COMMENTS
OHP					Off-highway parking is not permitted within the park
$ CCG					There are no commercial camp-grounds within this park. The nearest are at Moab, 33 miles northeast of the park
PCG	Dead Horse Point	Near visitor center; see campground description	All vehicles	U 313, park road	Inquire at visitor center concerning site availability
PC					No primitive camping of any sort is permitted within the park

Goblin Valley State Park

TYPE	NAME	LOCATION	ACCESS	ROUTE	COMMENTS
OHP					Off-highway overnight parking not permitted within the park
$ CCG					There are no commercial campgrounds within this park. The nearest are at Hanksville, 32 miles to the south
PCG	Goblin Valley	Near visitor center; see campground description	All vehicles	U 24 and park road	Dirt access road is rough and may be impassable to standard highway vehicles when wet
PC					Primitive camping from vehicles is not permitted within the park, but backpack camping may be permitted in remote areas; check with park rangers for current regulations

Green River State Park

TYPE	NAME	LOCATION	ACCESS	ROUTE	COMMENTS
OHP					Off-highway overnight parking is not permitted within the park
$ CCG					There are no commercial camp-grounds within the park. The nearest are in Green River, 1/2 mile to the north
PCG	Green River	Near entrance station; see campground description	All vehicles	I-70/U.S. 50 and park access road	Inquire at entrance station concerning site availability
PC					No primitive camping of any sort is permitted within the park except during special events when the overflow parking area may be used; check with park ranger for current regulations

Newspaper Rock State Historical Monument

TYPE	NAME	LOCATION	ACCESS	ROUTE	COMMENTS
OHP					Off-highway overnight parking is not permitted within the park
$ CCG					There are no commercial camp-grounds within the park. The nearest is at the entrance to Canyonlands National Park, 23 miles west
PCG	Newspaper Rock	Across the road from Newspaper Rock; see campground description	All vehicles	U 211 and park road	Limited number of sites and facilities; stream water requires purification
PC					This park is too small to permit any type of primitive camping

Wind Whistle Campground - Canyon Rims Recreation Area

Canyon Rims Recreation Area

TYPE	NAME	LOCATION	ACCESS	ROUTE	COMMENTS
OHP			All vehicles	U.S. 191, Needles Overlook Road, Anticline Overlook Road	Off-highway overnight parking is permitted within the recreation area except at the developed overlooks or near the campgrounds
$ CCG					There are no commercial campgrounds within this recreation area. The nearest are at Moab, 34 miles north, or Monticello, 20 miles south
PCG	Hatch Point	Near Anticline Overlook Road; see campground description	All except large recreation vehicles	U.S. 163, Needles Road, Anticline Overlook Road	Limited number of sites; no ranger on duty
PCG	Wind Whistle	Beside Needles Overlook Road; see campground description	All vehicles	U.S. 191 Needles Overlook Road	No ranger on duty, but may be a campground host
PC		Backcountry	Off-road vehicles and backpackers	Off-road vehicle trails and hiking routes	Primitive camping is permitted beside the established trails from off-road vehicles, and anywhere by backpackers

Newspaper Rock State Park

Abajo Mountains

TYPE	NAME	LOCATION	ACCESS.	ROUTE	COMMENTS
OHP			All vehicles	All public roads	Off-highway overnight parking is permitted beside all public roads that enter the national forest areas of the mountains, except near established campgrounds
$ CCG					There are no commercial campgrounds within these mountains; the nearest are in Monticello and Blanding
PCG	Buck-board	Just east of Monticello; see campground description	All except large recreation vehi-cles	US 191 and forest roads	Inquire at U.S. Forest Service office in Monticello concerning site availability and road conditions
PCG	Dalton Springs	Just east of Monticello; see description	All vehicles	US 191 and access road	Inquire at U.S. Forest Service office in Monticello concerning site availability
PCG	Devils Canyon	Adjacent to US 191 see description	All Vehicles	US 191 and access road	
PCG	Red Bluff	North of Blanding; see description	Small recreation vehicles and off-road vehicles	US 191, coun-try and forest roads	Inquire locally concerning road conditions before heading for this small campground

PC		Mountain back-country	Some highway vehicles, small recreation vehicles, off-road vehicles	US 191, U 95, U 211, various mountain roads and trails.	Primitive camping permitted beside the established forest roads and trails from vehicles, and anywhere by backpackers, except where otherwise posted

Henry Mountains

TYPE	NAME	LOCATION	ACCESS.	ROUTE	COMMENTS
OHP			All except large recreation vehicles	All public roads	Off-highway overnight parking is permitted beside all public roads that enter the mountains, except near established campgrounds
$ CCG					There are no commercial campgrounds within these mountains; The nearest are in Hanksville to the north or Bullfrog to the south
PCG	Lonesome Beaver	Mount Ellen vicinity; see campground description	Some highway vehicles, smaller recreation vehicles, off-road vehicles	U 24, U 95 and mountain roads	Accessible only to off-road vehicles when roads are wet

PCG	McMillan Springs	Mount Ellen vicinity; see campground description	Some highway vehicles, smaller recreation vehicles, off-road vehicles	U 24, U 95 and mountain roads	Accessible only to off-road vehicles when roads are wet
PCG	Starr Springs	Mount Hillers vicinity; see campground description	Some highway vehicles, smaller recreation vehicles, off-road vehicles	U 276 and mountain roads	Accessible only to off-road vehicles when roads are wet
PC		Mountain back-country	Some highway vehicles, smaller recreation vehicles, off-road vehicles	U 24, U 95, U 276, various mountain roads and trails	Primitive camping is permitted beside the established roads and trails from vehicles, and anywhere by backpackers, except as otherwise posted

La Sal Mountains

TYPE	NAME	LOCATION	ACCESS.	ROUTE	COMMENTS
OHP			All except large recreations vehicles	All public roads	Off-highway overnight parking is permitted beside all public roads that enter the mountains, except near established campgrounds
$ CCG					There are no commercial campgrounds within these mountains; The nearest are in Moab to the west
PCG	Buckeye	Beside Buckeye Reservoir; see campground description	Some highway vehicles, smaller recreation vehicles, off-road vehicles	U 46, Canopy Gap road, Geyser Pass trail	Accessible only to off-road vehicles when roads are wet; Alternate access from town of Paradox, Colorado
PCG	Oowah Lake	Beside Oowah Lake; see campground description	Some highway vehicles, smaller recreation vehicles, off-road vehicles	U.S. 191, Spanish Valley Road, Loop Road, Oowah Lake trail	Accessible only to off-road vehicles when roads are wet
PCG	Warner Lake	Beside Warner Lake; see campground description	Some highway vehicles, smaller recreation vehicles, off-road vehicles	U 128, Castle Valley Road, Loop Road, forest road	Accessible only to off-road vehicles when forest road is wet

PC		Mountain backcountry	Some highway vehicles, smaller recreation vehicles, off-road vehicles	U.S. 191, Utah 46, Utah 128, C90, C141, various mountain roads and trails	Primitive camping is permitted beside the established roads and trails from vehicles, and anywhere by backpackers, except as otherwise posted

Navajo Indian Reservation

TYPE	NAME	LOCATION	ACCESS	ROUTE	COMMENTS
OHP					Off-highway parking within the reservation is not recommended except as indicated on the various highway camping charts.
$ CCG		Monument Valley; see U.S. 163 camping chart	All vehicles	U.S. 191 and access road	Within the reservation area described in this book, there is only one commercial campground.
PCG	Navajo National Monument	Southwest of Kayenta	All vehicles	U.S. 160, A 564 and monument road.	Small National Park Service campground.
PC					Primitive camping within the reservation is by special permit only. For details, contact Navajo authorities.

Canyon Country Developed Campgrounds

Public Campgrounds

Name	Location & Nearest Highway
Buckboard	Abajo Mountains, U.S. 163
Buckeye	La Sal Mountains, Utah 46 or Colorado 90
Bullfrog	Lake Powell, Utah 276
Capitol Reef	Capitol Reef National Park, Utah 24
Dalton Springs	Abajo Mountains, U.S. 163
Dead Horse Point	Dead Horse Point State Park, Utah 313
Devils Canyon	Abajo Mountains, U.S. 163
Goblin Valley	Goblin Valley State Park, Utah 24
Goosenecks	Goosenecks State Reserve, Utah 261
Green River	Green River State Recreation Area, I-70 & U.S. 50
Halls Crossing	Lake Powell, Utah 263
Hatch Point	Canyon Rims Recreation Area, U.S. 163
Hite	Lake Powell, Utah 95
Hovenweep	Hovenweep National Monument,Utah 262
Lees Ferry	Glen Canyon National Recreation Area, U.S. 89A
Lonesome Beaver	Henry Mountains, Utah 24 or Utah 95
McMillan Springs	Henry Mountains, Utah 24 or Utah 95
Natural Bridges	Natural Bridges National Monument, Utah 95
Newspaper Rock	Newspaper Rock State Historical Monument, Utah 211
Oowah Lake	La Sal Mountains, U.S. 163
Red Bluff	Abajo Mountains, U.S. 163
Sand Island	San Juan River, U.S. 163
Squaw Flat	Canyonlands National Park, Utah 211
Starr Springs	Henry Mountains, Utah 276
Wahweap	Lake Powell, U.S. 89
Warner Lake	La Sal Mountains, Utah 128
Willow Flat	Canyonlands National Park, Utah 313
Windwhistle	Canyon Rims Recreation Area, U. S. 163

Further Reading

Visitors who wish to know more about the unique and fascinating canyon country of southeastern Utah will find other books and maps in the ***Canyon Country*** series both useful and informative.

General Information

Canyon Country **HIGHWAY TOURING** by F. A. Barnes. A guide to the highways and roads in the region that can safely be traveled by highway vehicles, plus descriptions of all the national and state parks and monuments and other special areas in the region.

Canyon Country **GEOLOGY** by F. A. Barnes. A summary of the unique geologic history of the region for the general reader, with a list of its unusual land-forms and a section on rock collecting.

Canyon Country **PREHISTORIC INDIANS** by Barnes & Pendleton. A detailed description of the region's two major prehistoric Indian cultures, with sections telling where to view their ruins, rock art, and artifacts.

Canyon Country **PREHISTORIC ROCK ART** by F. A. Barnes. A comprehensive study of the mysterious prehistoric rock art found throughout the region, with a section listing the places where it can be viewed.

Canyon Country **ARCHES & BRIDGES** by F. A. Barnes. An overview of the unique natural arches, bridges and windows found throughout the region, with hundreds depicted.

CANYONLANDS NATIONAL PARK - ***Early History & First Descriptions*** by F. A. Barnes. A summary of the early history of this uniquely spectacular national park, including quotes from the journals of the first explorers to see and describe it.

HIKING THE HISTORIC ROUTE of the 1859 MACOMB EXPEDITION by F. A. Barnes. A detailed guide to hiking the route of the first American expedition to enter southeastern Utah and describe the spectacular land now within Canyonlands National Park.

THE LABYRINTH RIMS - 60 Accesses to Green River Overlooks by Jack Bikers. Descriptions of most of the backcountry roads and off-road vehicle trails and scenic overlooks on both sides of the Green River.

BACKCOUNTRY GUIDE BOOKS AND MAPS

Canyon Country **HIKING & Natural History** by F. A. Barnes. A summary of the unusual natural history of the region, plus descriptions of most of the established trails and a sampler of trail-less routes.

Canyon Country **OFF-ROAD VEHICLE TRAILS - Arches and La Sals Areas** by F. A. Barnes.
Canyon Country **OFF-ROAD VEHICLE TRAILS - Island Area** by F. A. Barnes.
Canyon Country **OFF-ROAD VEHICLE TRAILS - Canyon Rims and Needles Areas** by F. A. Barnes.
Canyon Country **OFF-ROAD VEHICLE TRAILS - Maze Area** by Jack Bickers.
Canyon Country **OFF-ROAD VEHICLE TRAILS - Canyon Rims Recreation Area** by F. A. Barnes.
Each book contains descriptions of most of the backcountry roads and off-road vehicle trails in each region.

Canyon Country **OFF-ROAD VEHICLE TRAIL MAP - Arches and La Sals Areas** by F. A. Barnes.
Canyon Country **OFF-ROAD VEHICLE TRAIL MAP - Island Area** by F. A. Barnes.
Canyon Country **OFF-ROAD VEHICLE TRAIL MAP - Canyon Rims and Needles Areas** by F. A. Barnes.
Canyon Country **OFF-ROAD VEHICLE TRAIL MAP - Maze Area** by F. A. Barnes.
Canyon Country **OFF-ROAD VEHICLE TRAIL MAP - Canyon Rims Recreation Area** by F. A. Barnes.
Special topographic maps showing the roads and off-road vehicle trails in each area. Includes information on routes for mountain bikes.

Canyon Country **MOUNTAIN BIKING** by F. A. Barnes and Tom Kuehne. Background information useful to mountain bikers, detailed descriptions of 23 good trails for biking, and basic information about the other major trails in the canyon country region.

Canyon Country **RIVER RUNNING** by Verne Huser. Descriptions of all the rivers in southeastern Utah that can be boated by inflatables, kayaks, or canoes, plus information about access, equipment, and natural history.

Canyon Country **SLICKROCK HIKING & BIKING** by F. A. Barnes. Introduces an approach to hiking and biking that is unique to the canyon country of southeastern Utah, then describes and gives detailed directions for reaching many places where these new forms of recreational activity can be sampled.

UTAH-COLORADO MOUNTAIN BIKE TRAIL SYSTEM - Route I - Moab to Loma - "Kokopelli's Trail" by Peggy Utesch. A complete mile-by-mile guide to this 138-mile mountain bike trail, with elevation charts and additional useful information.

NOTES
FAVORITE CAMPING SPOTS